DIVORCED
BUT STILL DAD

The Faith Principles of Fatherhood for Divorced Men

Ken Gordon

ISBN 978-1-64003-046-6 (Paperback)
ISBN 978-1-64003-047-3 (Digital)

Covenant Books, Inc.
11661 Hwy 707
Murrells Inlet, SC 29576
www.covenantbooks.com

Reviewed By Joshua Soule for Readers' Favorite Review

Rating: 5 Stars

"You may be devastated by divorce because of bad character traits displayed by either you or your ex, but that doesn't give you the right to not live up to the expectations of your children." Ken Gordon has written a masterpiece—Divorced But Still Dad: The Faith Principles of Fatherhood for Divorced Men, a powerful piece of literature that provides guidance on how to be a father in the challenges of divorce. Divorced But Still Dad begins with Gordon accounting for his own personal experiences through a divorce, and the strategies he employed to continue to be a good father during this time. Gordon examines the potential reasons for a marriage to fail and follows up by providing guidance to divorce your spouse but not your children. Rev. Dr. Ken Gordon does not stop there, however; he intelligently articulates Bible-guided strategies for battling over property and financial assets, your role as a man as it pertains to your children and ex-spouse, handling the emotional trauma that will follow the divorce, and dating again the right way.

On a personal level, I could not have connected more to Divorced But Still Dad. Author Ken Gordon's education and experience undoubtedly shine through in his writing. I found Gordon's use of scripture alongside personal experiences to be very inspirational and motivating. As a divorced father myself, quotes such as "It is easy to make excuses and buckle under the weight of a difficult task, but God is calling you to be a provider, protector and priest" are just as powerful to me today as they would have been during my divorce. I encourage all divorced fathers to read Divorced But Still Dad; in fact, I encourage all fathers to read it. Ken Gordon has provided this much-needed guidance at a critical time. An excellent read!

CONTENTS

PREFACE

This book is based upon the real-life experiences of Ken Gordon Jr. The publisher and associated imprints, vendors, and retailers assume all association to names, places, and experiences the author presents in this book to be truthful and original. The author assumes all responsibility for inaccurate portrayal of events or activities that may be questioned or deemed factually incorrect. The author has agreed to indemnify the publisher, its imprints, vendors, and retailers from any liability or claims concerning the author's work.

DEDICATION

I dedicate this book to my son, Kenneth III, and my daughter, Cidnee Janae—two of the brightest beams of light in my life. The two of you inspire me to be a better Dad every day of my life.

FOREWORD

By Leslie Gordon

A good man leaves an inheritance to his children s children (Proverbs 13:22).

For Christians, divorce and destruction are synonymous in that there is a cataclysmic separation between a husband and wife which results in the ripping of flesh.

The covenant between man, woman, and God is broken. But, what about the children of divorce? What about their fundamental rights to experience love and have a relationship with both parents? What about the preservation of the Word of God within the home and family?

Rather than receive the Spiritual inheritance they are promised, children of divorce are often left with emotional wounds and pain so devastating that they are carried into adulthood and passed down from one generation to the next.

> *And thou shalt teach them diligently unto thy children, and shalt talk of them when thou sittest in thine house and when thou walkest by the way, and when thou liest down, and when thou risest up* (Deuteronomy 6:7).

The intentional and unintentional actions of divorcing parents which place children in the middle of conflict and provide them with less attention and support cause destruction so great that it can

11

nullify the inheritance. A good man does not leave his children as unloved, abandoned, living below his means, victims of manipulation, or without knowing Christ.

We must remember that children are not bystanders just watching the destruction of divorce occur; they are participants in the family and therefore deeply impacted by every decision. Understand that it is their God-given right to receive an inheritance; no one—including and especially parents—has the right to interfere with it.

My three-year divorce almost destroyed me physically, financially, and emotionally. It was not until I surrendered to God and allowed Him to fight my battles that my life began to move forward with a greater sense of peace, forgiveness, and direction. While God was doing a work in me, I was still single-handedly working to protect my children from the fallout of the divorce. As a mother, I needed to protect my babies.

Eventually, I realized that my protection only lasted up to the time my children walked out of the front door; it did not cover all of the perils confronting them, aiming to steal their inheritance.

My children and their inheritance needed greater protection than I could provide. I knew I needed to release my hold on them; allow their parental relationships to exist without my interference; release the guilt I carried that caused me to give in to their every desire despite my financial situation; and release the guilt that caused me to ease up on any necessary disciplinary actions.

Rather than continue on with Bionic Woman Heroics, I reconnected to the ultimate power source and set out to rebuild the inheritance that was rightfully due to my children and their children. Through fasting, praying, and soaking up the Word of God, I was able to fully release my children, their future, and my relationship with them into God's hands. I was assured and able to finally rest knowing their inheritance was fully protected wherever they were.

Train up a child in the way he should go: and when
he is old, he will not depart from it (Proverbs 22:6).

Proverbs 22:6 reminds me that nothing and no one can destroy the birthright of truth that I've helped instill in my children.

The magnitude of the inheritance referenced in the Bible is more than a gift of land or a life-insurance policy designating your child as the beneficiary. It is a gift than can pave the way to everlasting life for your child. It is a gift that holds the key to their success and the success of generations to come.

This Spiritual inheritance pays dividends early in a child's life and benefits later as parents exemplify righteous living and consistently teach the Biblical principles of unconditional love, grace, praise, worship, the joy of giving, and the Spirit of overcoming. It is so important for Spiritually mature parents to stay vigilant and not allow the fallout of divorce to emotionally damage their children nor compromise their ability to live a joy-filled life with both parents. A good man will always keep his children's heart in mind despite divorce.

This book is written by a man who cherishes the Living Word and his family. He is that good man who has already begun the Biblical teachings and setting of examples to leave an inheritance to our children.

Fathers, do not provoke your children to anger, but bring them up in the discipline and instruction of the Lord (Ephesians 6:4).

Ken is a father who relies on faith principles, to encourage and challenge our children to be all that God has called them to be. It is written by a man educated and humbled by the lessons of life, love, and divorce.

Knowing the importance of a child's inheritance, any man I entrusted with the care of my heart and my children had to have a strong relationship with God. It was also vitally important that he have positive relationships with his own children and his ex-wife or the mother of his children.

When I met Ken, our connection was powerful, and we both admit to pinching ourselves repeatedly after our first date. Our conversations were open, transparent, and long. We held nothing back, including our faith and the hurts and lessons from our failed marriages. Right away, I knew God was very much involved in our meeting because Ken possessed every standard for a husband that God had placed in my heart, including, and most importantly, being a believer in Christ.

> *Be ye not unequally yoked together with unbelievers: for what fellowship hath righteousness with unrighteousness? And what communion hath light with darkness* (2 Corinthians 6:14)?

Being more than a self-proclaimed believer; Ken is that good man who is obedient and wants God for who He is. He is that man who cherishes his children and respects his ex-wife.

My husband and I both understand that cultivating positive relationships is key to our success and that of our children and their children. While I know it is often difficult to retain a positive relationship with an ex-spouse after divorce, it was extremely important to me for any potential suitor to have a healthy co-parenting relationship with his ex-wife and/or the mother of his children.

> *Be kind to one another, tenderhearted, forgiving one another, as God in Christ forgave you* (Ephesians 4:32).

If a man has unforgiveness, revenge, or bitterness in his heart aimed toward the mother of his children, he is certainly not exemplifying Christ as his negative emotions threaten the inheritance and often overrule what is best for the children.

Successful co-parenting requires each parent to control their emotions and stay focused on the children and the next generation. It is my belief that the man who can show respect towards the mother of his children, if for nothing more than her position, and also teach his children to honor their mother is keeping the hope of the inheritance alive in his children. Ken is a great example of this good man who collaborates in co-parenting and keeps the hearts of his children in mind.

For every child who has experienced divorce and lost his/her inheritance, this book had to be written. It was written for me, my children, and yours. Yes, my inheritance was delayed due to my parent's divorce also. Now that I know what is at stake, I refuse to allow my children to go forth unprotected, building their lives on shaky foundations and living in darkness. It is my hope that my marriage to Ken will help to restore a sense of strength and provide a godly example of how our children can build strong houses of their own.

Ken is qualified to write this book because every day he works to please the Lord and give his best to me and our children. He may make mistakes, but he never gives up on God and getting it right. I admire and love him more each day for his commitment to God, our family, and the community.

While the choice to receive the inheritance belongs to our children, Ken and I will deliver the message. Despite our previous broken marriages, we are committed to leaving a godly inheritance to all four of our children. We pray this book will help you do the same for yours.

To any woman of divorce who happens to read this book, God's Word is for all to live by. I believe reading this book will help you to understand the feelings and duties of a divorced father and allow you to rethink your own co-parenting strategy.

> *For the Lord your God moves about in your camp to protect you and to deliver your enemies to you. Your camp must be holy, so that he will not see among you anything indecent and turn away from you* (Deuteronomy 23:14).

I encourage you to grow your faith and honor your children's right to have a relationship with their father without your interference. Entrust the care of your children to God as you also plan to leave a Spiritual inheritance to your babies and theirs. The Lord will bless your faithfulness.

INTRODUCTION

I am divorced. From that marriage came two children. I have an amazing daughter who is my princess. I have an awesome son who is incredible. These are my only two biological children. When I was a young man, I dreamed of having children. I wanted a daughter and I wanted a son. The truth is that I wanted more than two, but God blessed me with such awesome children there was no need to try to beat perfection. Am I saying my children are perfect? Thank God no. Am I saying I was a perfect Dad? Absolutely not.

Much like my Christian walk, I made many mistakes as a Dad. I was so far from perfect. I often tell my children that I want them to benefit from the mistakes I made in the past with the hope they will not repeat those same mistakes.

I continue to make every effort to be honest with my children about my imperfections and the mistakes I've made.

> *But grow in grace, and in the knowledge of our Lord and Saviour Jesus Christ* (2 Peter 3:18).

I believe the Scripture 2 Peter 3:18 is the epitome of my life as a Dad and my faith as a Christian. We are not perfect, but we are progressing.

I am progressing every day.

I am learning and unlearning.

Each day, I see ways to be a better Dad and a better person. By the grace of God, because of what I see, I am pursuing every opportunity to improve as a father to my two children.

Why did I write this book?

I wrote this book so others could identify with my struggles and failings and, hopefully, by God's grace, help others avoid those same pitfalls. I wrote this book because I have two wonderful children who I love with my entire heart but failed repeatedly. I am confident that no other father in this world can love his children more than I love mine. But I am also convinced that sharing my experiences as a Dad can help other men save their children from experiencing what my children endured.

Looking back and taking inventory of my many mistakes, I had no choice but to turn my attention to the Word of God for direction and guidance. It was during that process that I drew the inspiration for this book and the faith principles that helped me build an understanding of how I could be a better father. That process helped me analyze my personal humanity and the responsibility of being a real man.

> *All Scripture is given by inspiration of God, and is profitable for doctrine, for reproof, for correction, for instruction in righteousness* (2 Timothy 3:16).

What does God have to do with it?

As a Christian minister, I chose the Bible for my inspiration, but you may choose whatever source you find appropriate. There is no standard manual for being a father. When my children were born, there was no manual attached to their ankles; I had to search for one. I searched and did my best to prepare myself for the greatest responsibility of my life. After some time, I found that manual in the Bible.

You are free to accept or reject anything I say in this book, based on the Word of God. You are certainly free to decide you want to receive inspiration from some other source.

> *....but as for me and my house, we will serve the Lord* (Joshua 24:15).

However, as for me and for those of you who've decided to read this book, my learning process and teaching method is through the lens of God.

My personal disclaimer:
Throughout this book, I will reference Biblical principles and Scriptures in order to properly reinforce my message. The Bible is a vastly substantive book that provides multiple case studies that are applicable to the lessons I share with you on fatherhood.

The Scriptures I share with you are merely the ones that I've chosen to quote. Accordingly, this book is not meant to be an exhaustive guide or a step-by-step dictate; it is meant to stir up the Godly Man that may be undiscovered by men who are either divorced, separated or currently married. It is meant to inform women of what they should expect and how they can impact the relationship men have with their children.

Finally, I cannot stress enough that I am not perfect. I do not want you to think that my family is perfect because we are not. We are still growing in grace and learning from each other daily.

Please take the time to read my book; I encourage you to learn from my mistakes, receive inspiration from my sincere efforts and take reference to all I did to be Divorced, but still Dad.

CHAPTER 1

A SAD TRUTH

When I was a little boy, I dreamed of getting married and having children. I carefully planned my life: graduate from high school, graduate from college in four years, find a well-paying and secure career, get married, buy a house, have four children, save money to send them to college, and then grow old having lived the American dream.

In my mind, I created the perfect marriage. My wife would be everything a man would want in a wife—full of the surprises and the bonuses expected of your significant other.

Despite how important marriage was to me, I thought more about having children than I did about getting married. I wanted the opportunity to influence and shape a child's life from birth to adulthood. Though my parents were excellent and my childhood full of joy-filled memories, I still desired for children to have a better life than I had.

I knew my children would love me for me and not judge me, try to change me or criticize me. I wanted the unconditional agape love that comes from children. The thought of having my own children meant I could be myself, even if I wasn't the greatest person in the world. To them, I would be the greatest no matter what.

When I started crafting my life plans, I never thought about the potential of my marriage ending or what would happen if I had to get a divorce. That was nowhere near what I thought about.

I have hit for the cycle. My first marriage was a few years after college but it ended in annulment after only six months. It was devastating to know I was lied to, but it didn't stop me from pursuing my American Dream. I kept the faith.

Years later I married again. The marriage lasted only eleven months then my wife passed away. She died from AIDS. Did I know? I had no idea. Did she tell me? No she did not. She actually knew the whole time and that made it worse.

I could have been ready to throw my hands up and treat every woman I met with mistrust and suspicion. But I was still convinced the American dream was for me and I had not given up on having children! So, despite the lies and deceit of my second marriage, I pressed on. Optimistic. Believing.

Hopeful. I refused to punish anyone in my present for the sins of those in my past.

"Those were isolated incidents," I told myself. "Treat each person on their own merit."

So, I pressed on.

I did not give up searching for the woman I thought would help me be all I desired to be as a husband and father. Eventually, I remarried again. The marriage yielded the children I so badly wanted. However, I did not want children so badly I was willing to have them out of wedlock. I did not want children so badly I was willing to have them before I was financially able to support them. Yes, I wanted children, but with so precious a gift, I wanted them the right way.

I went to college and studied very hard. I committed myself to graduating before getting married and before having children. I committed myself to securing my professional foundation before having children. I really wanted children. I desperately sought after children I could protect, provide for and love. No matter how many times I failed at marriage, I was determined that one day I would have children.

That marriage, though ending after sixteen years, produced two of the most wonderful gifts God could have given me. The marriage ended in divorce, but the children are mine forever, and I, with all my warts, am theirs!

For almost half a century I watched other marriages end in divorce, just as mine had. I watched bliss turn to rage. I watched happy couples turn into hurtful individuals. I witnessed disappointment and defeat in the marriages of couples I counseled.

One couple I counseled seemed perfect for one another. He was a doctor and she was an attorney. I knew both of them before they married and even before they started dating. Their wedding was a fairy tale. The day was spectacular with over four hundred people attending. The newlyweds departed in a horse-drawn carriage. They were truly a perfect couple if I had ever seen one.

However, shortly after their wedding they came to me for counseling. By the way, when I say shortly, I mean shortly—one week after they came back from their two-week honeymoon.

When they reached out and asked to meet with me, I was befuddled. During our meeting, they shared that both were disillusioned and crestfallen.

How could they be so disillusioned after only two weeks?

They did not have children (thankfully) and their marriage ended shortly thereafter. So much for the perfect couple.

So, what was it that made them date for several years, then get married, then less than a month later, call it quits? Whatever the catalyst, they both turned into bitter and vengeful people, who could not stand the sight of one another. Considering the way in which their marriage fell apart, it was a great thing they did not have children.

Then there was the couple that was the living epitome of Barbie and Ken. He was a corporate salesman and she was an administrative professional. They had three children that seemed oddly independent—appearing to lack the requisite parental engagement.

Observation of the children illustrated there was little interaction between the children and their father. He was always working. When he was not working, he was golfing with his buddies. When he was not working or golfing, he was taking clients out to lunch and dinner. Not surprisingly, they ended up coming to me for counseling. While I hate to admit it, by the time they got to me, the die had already been cast. He was not going to change, because he did not see a reason to do so. He was married and did not want to divorce his spouse. Unfortunately, he was more married to his job than to his wife. His wife was expendable. His children were expendable. His job was not. Or at least, that is how he saw it and how he behaved. His job was his real spouse.

His children, two boys and a girl, cried out for attention and to be part of his world. However, he had already made up his mind. He was getting divorced so he could be faithful to his true love—his job. It seemed in his mind, his children would only slow him down.

Again, when I first met this couple, I would have never dreamed they would one day end up at each other's throats over who gets the barbeque grill and who gets to keep the painting that was hanging over the sofa!

One of the seminal questions is how does this happen? How do happy couples turn into such hateful individuals?

While that may only be evaluated properly on a case-by-case basis, there are certain common threads I have seen in my ministerial counseling.

Seven Reasons Why Marriages Fail

Common "marriage killers" I have encountered in my counseling are disappointment, delusion, selfishness, abandonment, dissimilarity, inability to communicate and misguided initial intentions.

1. Disappointment – They are not who you thought they were. They are who you'd hoped they were not. They cannot be who you want them to be.
2. Delusion – What happened to the fairy tale life? What happened to the perfect spouse, the American Express and the 2.5 children? What happened to happily ever after?
3. Selfishness – Infidelity. Substance abuse. Hanging on to the past or to a single lifestyle. Refusal to mature and carry their weight in the marriage. Desire to keep things separate. No shared responsibility or commitment. Disconnected with the needs of the spouse. Emotionally unavailable.

4.   Abandonment – Not contributing to the needs of the household. Never around. Always working. Married to job. Married to family (parents, siblings, etc.).

5.   Dissimilar – Going in different directions. Wanting different things in life. One person is ambitious, the other is lazy. Unequally yoked.

6.   Inability to communicate – Constantly arguing, yet never resolving. Shutting down. Marital silence. Inability of one person to raise a concern without the other turning the tables. One person who never sees themselves. One person who is never wrong. One person who can never apologize or admit being wrong. One person who is a professional debater, while the other detests confrontation.

7.   Misguided initial intentions – Marrying to be rescued. Using marriage to improve social status. Gold diggers. Trophy wives. Lust. Sexually motivated intent. Social acceptance.

While there are other reasons, these are the most common I have encountered during my counseling. In all the above situations, the end result normally produces myriad negative emotions. At the end of the day, just about every marriage that ends in divorce, contains a strong element of disappointment. How we deal with disappointment is at the crux of the matter. Our ability to struggle to our feet and stand up, wobbly legs and all, is what makes the difference.

Yes, you can lie on your back cursing the blow that sent you reeling. Or, you can struggle to your feet, shake it off and walk away with your head held high—even if you have a black eye!

The sooner you get up, dust yourself off, forgive yourself, forgive the other person and introspectively put it all into perspective, the better the chances you will not become hurtful to others.

The people that came to me generally came so I could help them determine if they had a chance or if they were too far gone. Some came under the pretense of "working on their marriage," but the truth is they were there to work on their divorce.

During my Christian counseling sessions, I worked with couples to determine the Biblical basis for their conflict and through Biblical reflection and prayer, determine their best course forward. However, I will readily admit, if they came to me with two outs in the ninth inning and no desire to get back in the batter's box, I am no miracle worker and God will not make a person change their mind. If they came to me to work on their divorce, I did all I could to accommodate them! And in that accommodation, I kept my eyes trained on the children and did all I could, through my counseling, to salvage the children and their psyche.

During my Christian counseling sessions, what I saw was that some couples fell out of love. And others did not fall, they were pushed. Some couples outgrew one another. And some couples set the bar so high they did not have a prayer of succeeding.

The picture painted by society (including the media and our parents) is that love is all you need to make a marriage work. We have been led down a primrose path, chock full of songs and movies that repeated the chorus that "love is all you need."

However, the truth is love is only the beginning of what you need. Friendship, compatibility, communication, trust, honesty, freedom to be who you are, patience and restraint are equally important to a successful marriage. Love does not displace those things, it augments them.

When I was in college I dated a wonderful young lady. She was beautiful and vibrant. She was the same "yoke" as me. She and I had a lot in common. She had strong feelings for People thought we were perfect for each other.

However, there was one major problem: I was unhappy. I did not know why.

I just knew I was not happy.

I called my mother and told my mother how I felt.

"Mom, I know I love her. She is a wonderful person. But I do not want to be with her. How can that be?"

My mother told me something I will never forget:

"Just because you love someone does not mean things will work out and you will be together." I was astounded.

But how can that be? Love is supposed to conquer all. How many song writers said it in their songs? How many movies ended with that conclusion? It didn't follow the path society embraced, yet, I knew she was right. I loved that young lady, but that is where it stopped. Perhaps I loved only with my eyes. Perhaps I loved with my personality. Perhaps I loved with my emotions. Whatever it was, it was not enough. What I now understand is love is not enough. If your relationship is not of God, it won't matter how much you care for someone.

When people love with their eyes and their loins, it should be no surprise that after a while their eyes grow dim and their loins go soft. After all, even with Viagra, you are only guaranteed to last for four hours and after that, you better call a doctor.

My minister's hat tells me to say people should wait until after marriage before introducing sex into the relationship. The Bible refers to sex before marriage as fornication, and while some people find the Bible hard to grasp and outdated, I can tell you that fornication before marriage has the potential to compromise the marriage and confuse feelings.

Sex bonds a man and woman together in holy matrimony and seals the marriage ceremony. It was never meant to be casual and recreational. If we are being guided by our loins and libido, we should expect misdirection of emotion. It is reasonable to accept that we are guided by what feels good. We are guided by what we like. Our humanism (flesh) responds favorably to pleasure, negatively to pain and violently to ennui. Therefore it is understandable why we become awash in the pleasurable feelings of sex and misdiagnose those pleasure sensors as being love sensors.

When we allow our loins to guide us we confuse two very powerful sensations as being synonymous. Then later down the line, after time and life provide a differentiation between the two, disappointment and dismay set in. That reality leads to divorce being emotionally, mentally and psychologically draining and destructive to family after family. While those two senses are intertwined and confused, everything might appear perfect. Then comes the challenges, children, responsibilities, extra pounds, job pressures, the stress of life and all the outside forces that tease out sexual pleasure from love. When our eyes are finally opened and we see ourselves and the other person for who and what they are, it can be like an airplane being shot out of the sky. Some may be fortunate to have parachutes, but most will be doomed to crashing down to earth in a fiery ball.

Many, who did not have wise counsel, allowed libido and loins to lead them into relationships that ended badly years later. That is how it works when one bases their marriage and future on something as temporary as an erection.

Temporary may be three minutes for some, and thirty minutes for others. Regardless of whether it is three minutes or thirty minutes, once it is over, it will not take long before you forget how great it felt. All you will remember is what was not done for you lately.

The same applies to the plight of marriages. Whether the marriage lasts three years or thirty years, once it is over, it is over. And all you know is you are lying there in the wet spot it produced thinking, "I really need to get up and take a shower."

Okay, I know what you are thinking. Once it's over, it's over? Take a shower? Explode into a fiery ball? For heaven's sake, why even take the leap? Geez, why even get married?

> *Whoever finds a wife finds a good thing and obtains favor of the Lord* (Proverbs 18:22).

> *Marriage is honorable…* (Hebrews 13:4)

> *Whoever finds a wife of noble character is blessed? She is worth far more than rubies. Her husband has full confidence in her and lacks nothing of value. She brings him good, not harm, all the days of her life* (Proverbs 31:10–13).

Marriage is sacred, honorable, and blessed—but only when done God's way. Marriage and sex are gifts from God that complement one another. They are not meant to be solo experiences entered into lightly, and they certainly are not meant to be a recreational activity.

I speak not from wistful conjecture but actual experience. As I said before, I have hit for the cycle. While I am not proud of that and do not wish it upon any other man or woman it is the narrative of my life. It is a life from which I cannot run and do not waste time regretting, rather I choose to use it as a platform to inform the decisions of those who are willing to listen and contemplate its usefulness regarding their own situations. One of my pastors used to say, "With life, you have to learn to swallow the meat and spit out the bones." I offer my diversity of experience as either meat or bones for you to chew upon. You can decide whether you swallow some of what I say or spit it out.

The Sanctity of Marriage

There is sanctity to marriage. There is blessedness to holy matrimony, but if you are divorcing, I submit to you the way you exit a marriage can be just as important as the way you entered. When it is over, and I'm not arguing your motives or reasons, but once it is over, one must be even more respectful of its sanctity than when you entered.

Here is what I mean:

When someone passes away, all their friends gather and have a somber ceremony. They honor the life of the person. They say good things. They eulogize the person.

Eulogy is derived from the Classical Greek word eulogia, which means "praise." It means a speech or writing in praise of a person, especially one who recently died. During this sacred period, everyone gets up and talks about their wonderful, and nostalgic memories of the deceased. Why? Because it is more important how you remember a person than how the person actually was. You choose not to remember the negative parts of the person, even if there was not much more to them than the negative.

I have yet to attend or preach a funeral where people got up and spoke ill of the person. Even if the person was a real jerk. People understand that our final thoughts of a person inform our eternal opinions and feelings. So, when you decide to exit a marriage, you should do the same thing. It is how you exit the marriage that will inform your children's opinion of themselves and their view of marriage in the future. The very construct of their marital psyche is informed by the withdrawal and exit strategy you implement.

As you exit your marriage or because you have exited your marriage, eulogize it. Do not denigrate the marriage no matter how terrible or unhappy it made you.

Eulogize, do not villainize.

Though it may be over, choose to remember the good.

That is not to say you are going to get back with the person or want to. It is to say you must allow your treatment of the divorce to inform your children's future.

Do not allow yourself to be caught up in the emotion of a failed marriage.

Do not allow stinkin' thinkin' to guide your treatment of the divorce. When you begin to ask yourself, "why?" When you begin to wonder, "how?"

When you begin to peer through a foggy, cloudy lens, you will begin to think how you were once so passionately in love. You remember how you once twirled around on the dance floor in front of all your family and friends. You recall how you once stood in front of the preacher taking serious vows, and now cannot stand the mention of the other's name.

The blissful became the bitter.

The happy became the hurtful.

This post-relationship analysis can cause you to exit and not provide the honor for the good the marriage produced.

This sad turn of events is amazingly common and routine. Though sad, perhaps it would not be as serious if children were not involved.

Okay, so maybe you go through this vicious cycle and there are no children? It might not have been good, and probably very unpleasant. But with only two people who both profess to be adults, it will not be as catastrophic as if you had children. When there are children involved, the stakes are much higher.

Exiting a marriage and regarding it as failed or a mistake can have a powerfully negative affect on everything associated with the marriage. When children are involved, you are planting a cancerous seed which will grow for generations beyond.

When you exit a marriage and allow the negative to be the predominant and final narrative, it is like planting radioactive waste deep in your children. As time goes on, that radioactive material will eat away at their insides and eventually destroy them internally—negatively affecting everything about who they are.

Allowing the negative impact of exiting a marriage to be the predominant and final narrative is like the people in Flint, Michigan, who for years drank dirty and tainted water. They now live with serious health complications and issues that will forever affect them. All because they drank dirty water. Do not force your children to drink the dirty water of your divorce. Filter it. Eulogize it.

Unfortunately, the sad truth is that too many children are negatively affected by parents, who profess to be adults, profess to be educated, profess to be mature and profess to be enlightened. Yet, when it comes to matters of the heart, the head goes out the window.

We cannot justify our actions with the tired line, "But he/she hurt me!" As if being hurt justifies reversion to childhood. As if being hurt gives permission to ignore your age, maturity, responsibility and enlightenment. Amazingly, the smartest and seemingly most mature people revert to playground bullies when they are hurt.

Be angry, yet do not sin (Ephesians 4:26).

So, you are hurt and angry. You are disappointed and dismayed. Maturity, education, and the God in you, dictate you sin not. It is not the sin towards one another for which I write this book and intercede, rather the sins we commit against our children.

I too have experienced divorced.

I went through the cycle of understanding it was over and there was no prospect for reconciliation. I attended individual and couple's therapy. I tried to stay "for the sake of the children." I scolded myself for being selfish and putting my happiness over that of my children's. I suppressed my discontent and tried to convince myself that my unhappiness was less important than my children growing up in a two-parent household.

I told myself I did not want my children to be a statistic—a media story of another African-American broken household, with the children being raised by a single mother. I told myself I had my opportunity for life and now it was my children's turn. I told myself everything I could think of to make myself stay. But in the end, none of those personal conversations were enough to make me stay.

For my own sanity and happiness, I needed to get divorced. I did not blame my ex; she is a wonderful person, but we just were not good as husband and wife. I do not begrudge the fact that we grew apart or that we wanted different things from life. I do begrudge the fact that we were not equally yoked. Instead I celebrate the fact that our union produced two remarkable children! I understand that my children are made up of equal parts of me and equal parts of her. So, why would I curse her, thus cursing part of my own children? Never. My children deserve to believe that every part of them is wonderful, not just the part that is made up of me.

Do Not Divorce Your Children

Not long ago a woman came to me for counsel.

This woman was full of life. I saw the God in her. She was kind, caring, loving and thoughtful. She shared the events that led to the demise of her marriage and ultimately her divorce. I listened in amazement as she shared the abuse and disrespect she endured during and after her marriage. She shared how her ex treated her and their children, post-divorce. It was hard enough to hear her speak about how she was treated by her ex, but hearing how he treated the children was even harder. It was as if he was divorcing them too.

It was important for me to hear his side of the story, so I met the ex-husband. Our conversation revealed obvious divergent perspectives of what went wrong in their relationship, yet one thing stuck out to me. I was bothered by the fact that he had become totally disengaged from his children. It was as if he was no longer their dad. He would not go see them play sports nor send them gifts on their birthdays. He would not acknowledge them during the course of the year. He walked away from the marriage and all that it produced in order to pursue his own happiness and "do his thing."

The man wanted to be single again. He wanted to date and sleep around with younger women—of which he had felt deprived during his 20-year marriage. He was tired of his 50-something wife with her belly fat and cellulite, as he put it.

Never mind that the belly fat came from producing three wonderful children. Never mind that the cellulite came from her sacrificing herself and her body for the good of a clean house, children who were waited on hand and foot, dinner that was always cooked and a second job that helped pay the bills. Never mind that the extra weight came because she did not spend time in the gym, though she would have loved to do so, rather spending time catering to the needs of her family. But, in his mind, none of that mattered.

"Other women can do it, why can't you?" he insisted.

During counseling on more than one occasion, he stressed that he sees lots of women their age who are in great shape. Therefore, his dissatisfaction turned to resentment and then to anger.

By the way, did I mention that he was not a hard body? Did I mention that he had a few extra pounds? Yeah, neither did he.

After counseling this couple and seeing his contempt for his marriage, his ex and his children, I began doing research and speaking to more and more people about how many men react and respond to divorce, as it relates to the children. I looked at how men viewed the price they would have to pay for pursuing their happiness. I then looked at my own attitude and journey. I wrote this book because through the grace of God, I was able to figure out that the price for me pursuing my happiness was to ensure the mental, physical, psychological and natural well-being of those who did not ask to be in the middle—my children.

I wrote this book because I understand that fatherhood does not end the day the divorce is final.

I wrote this book because I wanted to speak to those men who allow anger, pride, hurt, guilt and indignation to cloud their eyesight and judgment.

Your marriage failed. You were likely unequally yoked or you just grew apart or perhaps your eyesight grew dim or your loins grew soft.

Whatever the reason, you made a decision that it was time to cut your losses and move on. Maybe she initiated it. Maybe you initiated it. Maybe you were in the wrong.

The truth is, it does not matter. Whatever the circumstances regarding your divorce or separation, the sooner you forgive yourself and your ex-wife, the sooner you will be able to heal and move on with your life.

CHAPTER 2

EQUALLY YOKED

I am happier than I have ever been. I am mentally healthy. I am psychologically whole. I am equally yoked. God is blessing my ministry and my household. So, how did I get here? What was the formula that allowed me to survive divorce and remember my commitment to my children while also focusing on my commitment to myself?

The balancing act was not an easy one.

There were days when I felt I failed. There were days when every indication was that all my plans, strategies and intents were nothing but fluff and garbage.

> *I can do all this through him who gives me strength* (Philippians 4:13).

> *...all things work together for good to them that love God, to them who are the called according to his purpose.* (Romans 8:28).

> *And David was greatly distressed; for the people spake of stoning him, because the soul of all the people was grieved, every man for his sons and for his daughters: but David encouraged himself in the Lord his God* (I Samuel 30:6).

I knew this was my source of strength during the times when my faith was challenged, when I cried until I could not cry anymore, when people were talking about me, and even when I found myself disappointed in my own situation.

The Divorce Struggle

I struggled for several years with whether or not I should actually get a divorce. More than any other reason, I vacillated because of my children. What would they think? How would they handle me and their mother getting a divorce? How would my children handle the shame and embarrassment? I accused myself of being selfish. I hated myself for wanting to leave but I had reached a point of no return. Finally, I discussed divorce with my children's mother and we both sat our children down and broke the news to them.

I had major work done on my house to ensure it would be a place my children could call home and a place where my children would be proud to have their friends visit. I worked hard not to allow emotion and pettiness to cloud the picture. I tried hard to be kind to my ex. I tried to be generous, figuring that for my children's sake, it was better to err on the side of being generous, than to err on the side of being stingy. I challenged myself to be a man and to be bigger than the situation. I hired a legal firm that specialized in representing men. It seemed like the right thing to do at the time. In retrospect, it was not the right thing for me. The attorney was used to dealing with vampires, who were out to suck the blood out of their wayward husbands. They were used to dealing with women who wanted to make their exes pay and pay big. I understood that, but was not prepared for the cut throat tactics they attempted to employ.

I did not want a war. I did not want surgical strikes. I did not want hand to hand combat. I wanted out of the marriage, not out of my children's life! However, it was very clear to me, that just as my attorney was gearing up for an all-out war, so too, was my ex's attorney. Because I made significantly more money than my ex and had more advanced education, it was seen as something of a David vs. Goliath. As I stood looking across the battlefield (courtroom) and watching out for rocks, I decided I did not want or need this route. What I needed was to sit down and talk to my ex. I needed to explain that though she was hurting, I was not trying to injure her. I needed to explain that I wanted to co-parent our children and if she would agree to a detente, I would abide by its strictures.

So, it was. I fired my blood thirsty attorney and instead used the money to buy each of my children new bedroom sets and flat screen TVs. Let me just state, objectively, I am fully aware of the need for attorneys such as the firm I hired. While they may not have been the right one for me, it does not mean I do not understand they are oft times necessary. I just wonder if there were greater communication, openness, contrition and transparency, would there be as much need for such a firm.

Nonetheless, after working so hard to do all the right things, I moved out and bought a house nearby. Then something crazy happened. My children all of sudden wanted nothing to do with me. They refused to come to my house. They did not want to talk to me on the phone. They shared stories with others about me and terrible things I did to their mother. All of a sudden, their mother was Mother Theresa and I was Satan incarnate.

I was devastated! After all I did? After being so generous? After stepping up to the plate as opposed to running away? This is what you do to me? I was insulted and angry. Friends told me to sit my children down and defend myself. Tell them your truth. Do not let them believe everything they are being told. Force them to come to your house, after all, you are their father! Depression set in. Frustration set in. Anger set in. I missed my children and desperately wanted to tell my side of the story. You know how people say they were down in the dumps? What is below the dumps? Because that is where I was.

But, sometimes you have to encourage yourself. So, during those tough times, those dark days, I did just that. I encouraged myself. I looked forward believing I would get through my period of darkness and emerge into the light. I kept the faith. I believed if I did the right thing, for the right reasons, God would smile on me and eventually I would get through the tough times and look back on all of it with a smile.

And you know what? That is exactly what happened. I never lost sight of my commitment to my children. I never lost sight of the fact that although I was divorced, I was still Dad to my children. Does that mean there was no pain? No. Does that mean my children skated through without any scars? No. It just means I tried to do all I could to mitigate their pain, angst and hurt. It meant I never lost sight of my responsibility to protect and provide for my children.

So, I wandered out of a marriage into divorce and into other relationships. While my children cannot tell you exactly how many "other relationships", more on that later, suffice it to say sometimes we look for comfort in the wrong set of arms. And, I certainly did that. However, I was grounded enough to know that searching for an antidote to the pain of divorce in another person's arms or between their legs or in their bed was never going to heal the pain I was feeling. The pain I was feeling was only going to be healed by running into the open arms of Jesus. While I know some people who read this may not be "religious" and may not believe in the power of Christ, I encourage you to read on. I am not proselytizing; I am merely sharing with you what it took to get me through.

But I digress. I did not find the perfect woman and that person with whom I was equally yoked until I took time to work on my relationship with God. I took some alone time and time to hear His voice.

I needed to do this coming out of a divorce and subsequent poor relationship choices.

Sometimes we jump out of the frying pan and into the fire, while trying to convince ourselves it is not as hot and we are not getting burned as bad. Often, because of relationship fatigue, where we are tired of relationship after relationship, we buy into the adage that a dissatisfying relationship is better than no relationship at all. After all, it was not bad all the time. Just on the days that ended in y. I found myself making poor choices and not listening to God. The bottom line is I had not taken time to grieve and heal. As a result, just like an open wound, if you do not cover it, apply antiseptic and give it time to heal, it can quickly get infected. Open wounds are more susceptible to infection than ones that are healed. Ones that are healed may leave scars, but they are not easily infected. As a matter of a fact, those scars create excess tissue, making it harder for infection to enter. So, here I was. I was an open wound, not healed and allowing bacteria to enter my life and cause an infection. I had not given myself time to heal and I was paying dearly for it through my poor post-divorce relationship choices.

Had I given myself time and allowed God to choose for me, my wounds would not be infected. God knows the right people for us. He knows who will help promote healing and he knows who is an opportunistic infection, looking for an open wound. Instead of waiting on God, waiting on my healing and waiting on my body to recover, I jumped out and picked my own mates.

However, somehow I survived and made it through, but by now I was convinced I was lousy at picking my own mate, so it was time I allowed God, who made me, knew everything about me and understood the plans he had for me, to pick the right person for me.

> *"For I know the plans I have for you," declares the Lord, "plans to prosper you and not to harm you, plans to give you hope and a future"* (Jeremiah 29:11).

So how did I allow God to help me pick a mate? First, I repented and admitted I needed help. No one can be helped until they admit they need help. So the first step was confession. The second step was to seek after God.

> *But seek ye first the kingdom of God, and his righteousness; and all these things shall he added unto you* (Matthew 6:33).

You must put God first. You must make your relationship with God the most important relationship to you. There is a saying that "if you take care of God's business, he will take care of yours." That saying is true.

I stopped thinking about myself and began thinking about my God. I stopped obsessing over a relationship and instead started seeking God and seeking to have a relationship with God. I prayed. I spent alone time. I read my Bible. I focused on healing. I started seeing a therapist. I was fully focused on inner healing and a Spiritual renewal. I stopped looking for someone to make me feel better and started focusing on making myself feel better. I did this by reading, working out, meditating.

I became aggressively introspective. During my alone time I asked myself tough questions. I looked closely at my habits, practices and behaviors. I asked myself why. Why did you get into that relationship? Why didn't you get out of that relationship? Why have you gotten into these situations in the past? Why, why, why? As I asked myself the tough "why" questions, I added prayer to that questioning. I asked God to help me answer those questions. There is something powerful about prayer. Call it mediation. Call it what you will, but when you talk to God, he answers!

So, I asked God to forgive me. I asked Him to forgive me for my sins. I asked Him to forgive me for leaving him out of my selection process. I asked him to forgive me for disregarding His warnings. I asked Him to forgive me for not trusting Him. I asked him to forgive me for not forgiving myself. I asked him to help me forgive myself. This is critical. The beginning of all healing is inner forgiveness. Before you can ever extend external forgiveness, you must have inner forgiveness. All healing starts with self-forgiveness.

Next I asked him to heal me from the inside out. I asked him to heal my pain and hurt. I asked him to heal my heart and my Spirit. I needed complete healing. I wanted to be whole for my children. I wanted to be complete for the relationship He had in store for me.

Finally, I asked him to restore me. I asked for restoration to Him. I asked for restoration to health and well-being. I needed this mentally and psychologically. I wanted to be mentally complete and whole for what lay ahead of me. I could not continue looking back, trying to see my hurt and pain in that little bitty mirror. I needed God's help to look forward through that huge windshield.

As I spent dedicated time alone with God, as I meditated on internal healing and improvement, and as I prayed for complete healing, a funny thing happened: God placed a beautiful angel into my life. He led me to her. It was not on purpose. I was not "looking for a wife," I found a wife. I found her because God led me to her. He led me to her because I took time to work on my relationship with Him.

Could I have found another relationship by just going out and hitting the clubs, bars and supermarkets? Sure. But, would I have found the person God had for me without taking time to seek Him first and get closer to Him? I do not believe I would have.

If you have been hurt. If you are coming out of a divorce. If you are coming out of a difficult and painful relationship. I encourage you to take several months off from dating, spend time alone focusing on getting to know yourself. Ask God for forgiveness, healing and restoration. Spend time seeking God. If you do, I am confident God will reward you with an Angel of your very own!

And He did just that for me!

Through taking time off from relationships and focusing on The Primary Relationship, God was able to heal me and prepare me for the person, for whom He had been preparing me all my life. After spending alone time, my perspective was not clouded, my vision was clearer, my senses were keener and my discernment was more acute. I was able to be led by the Spirit of God, instead of by my eyes or loins.

CHAPTER 3

SUBSTANCE OVER SURFACE

Make the right selection. Looking back on where I went wrong in my marriage, I know it was in my selection process. I allowed my eyes, and quite frankly, my body, to choose my companion. I was not led by God. I did not seek Him for the right mate. Instead, I had my checklist and nowhere on it was anything Spiritual. Okay, let's see, she needs to be between 5'3" and 5'5". She needs to be a "C" cup. She needs to have pretty hands and feet. She needs to have a short, sexy hairdo. The list went on and on. Pretty pathetic, huh? No wonder I ended up in Divorce Court later in my life. I was all about surface. I was all about what was pleasing to the eye. I remember growing up listening to The Commodores' song "Brick House." I'm sure you remember, "36/24/36, what a winning hand, owww." Song after song extolled the physical characteristics, while few mentioned the more important inner characteristics. Our society is obsessed with outward beauty. Television, movies, videos; they barrage us with images of "perfection." They direct us towards those who are physically attractive, while marginalizing character qualities.

Consequently, I fell prey. In my relationships, I looked for the nice legs, the flat stomachs and the perky breasts. I looked for the hour glasses and eschewed the pears. I believe if you are looking first on the outside, you are likely to overlook and minimize, or perhaps even discount the character. Further, I believe if you are too focused on the surface, as I was, beautiful women with substance will not want YOU anyway!

20/20 Character Vision

There is a tangible value to vision correction. Many men need corrective lenses or some super thick bifocals, to better view potential mates. Everyone has character. According to Merriam Webster, the definition of character is "the way someone thinks, feels, and behaves." I have also heard people say character is what you do, and who you are when no one is looking.

Everyone develops character through traits or underlying values that sum up the core of who we are. Examples of types of character traits include: honesty, loyalty, devotedness, love, kindness, and sincerity.

Some character traits can be bad like dishonesty, disloyalty, disrespect, greed, and selfishness.

When you compare and contrast the good and bad character traits of people in your life, what jumps out the most is the importance of knowing people in order to best evaluate their character. People can put up a facade and pretend they are a certain way or have a certain character trait.

20/20 Character Vision is that patient examination and careful attention paid to the spoken and unspoken, shown and hidden aspects of a person. Observance of reactions and responses most people do not notice is critical to the examination. It is that third eye that sees a person's real reactions to circumstances, situations, issues and challenges. Unfortunately, most men disregard the value of this attentive review.

> *Man looks on the outward appearance hut the Lord looks on the heart* (1 Samuel 16:7).

> *Above all else, guard your heart; for everything you do flows from it.* (Proverbs 4:23).

God uses 20/20 Character Vision when he looks at us because he looks at our hearts and not just at our outward appearance or performance. God is the model for how one develops 20/20 Character

Vision. One must look inward at a person. One must look at another's heart.

So how do you do that? The Lebanese Poet, Khalil Gibran said, "To understand the heart and mind of a person look not at what he has already achieved, but at what he aspires to."

So, if you are to look inward at a person, you would look not at what they say. You would not look at what they do. You would look at what they aspire to. You look at who they aspire to be. When you are looking at a person with 20/20 Character Vision you are seeing them, not as they are, but as they wish to be. You are looking at the person not for who you want them to be, but for who they want to be and who they are willing to work towards becoming.

Too many times, people get into relationships and they use "I-sight." They see the person according to themselves. They see the person according to who they want them to be. They see the person, based on what "I" want, not based on what the person is capable of being or wants to be. Yes, the antithesis to 20/20 Character vision is "I-sight" and it is a killer! You wake up 5, 10, or 20 years later, and your "I-sight" has dimmed and you are now disappointed. Character is the permanent part of who a person is and it does not grow old, it does not forget the lie it was acting out and it does not lose patience. That is why 20/20 Character Vision is critical. When you look at a person with 20/20 Character Vision, you are seeing the best of what is in them, but you are also seeing the worst. You are seeing the totality of a person and not just what appeals to you.

I learned a lesson a long time ago from a wonderful friend of mine. His name is Kinji and he and I met when I lived in Kansas City. When we first met, we were both in our twenties. Kinji was a preppy dressing, BMW driving, rap loving, basketball playing African-American from Oakland. I was a corporate dressing, company car driving, jazz loving, basketball participating African-American from New Jersey. We had nothing in common. The kinds of women he liked, I did not. The kind of job he had was different from mine. The way he dressed was markedly different from the way I dressed. I was not into rap. I was not into anything he was into. But we hit it off. We formed a friendship of opposites that has lasted almost thirty years. Recently, Kinji came to Delaware to be a Groomsman in my wedding and I was honored to have the support of such a wonderful friend. He would have been my Best Man, but I asked my Dad to do me the honor of being my Best Man and my Dad agreed.

Because of our differences, people would ask how Kinji and I got along. Where Kinji was concerned, I was determined to look at him with 20/20 Character Vision. And to that effect, Kinji was (and is) a man of amazing character. To this day, he still likes his Heineken and preppy clothes. Still likes his rap music and nice cars (although he has lowered himself to driving a Mercedes-Benz instead of a BMW). And he still thinks he can ball. But, among everything, this man still has amazing character. It is not about the outward man, it is about the inward man. I made a conscious decision with regards to our relationship. And here is the lesson Kinji taught me, and it is a lesson about 20/20 Character Vision.

Kinji taught me that when you meet a person you have three choices: 1) do not accept them for who they are and try to change them; 2) accept them for who they are and complain about them incessantly and in perpetuity; or 3) accept them for who they are, do not try to change them and do not complain about the person they are. It was a lifetime lesson for a 20-something young man.

You must look at the heart of a person—the part of your anatomy that cannot lie and does not change. If what you see is good, you accept them for who they are and love them as God loves us: purely, genuinely and unconditionally.

Love them and accept them, without complaining! If you can't do that, then love them but move on. No use complaining or trying to change people. Just move on. Make both of your lives easier.

So that is where so many of us mess up. We get into relationships and do not look at the person with our 20/20 Character Vision. We do not see the heart of the person. We do not see that thing in them that we can love forever, because it is who they are forever. Instead, we look at outward, impermanent and shallow things. We look at skin color, breast size, the size of the onion, at feet, and at hair. We look at what they drive or where they work. All these things are subject to change overnight. Many men need corrective lenses that will allow them to look beyond topical and surface accoutrements. Corrective lenses allow you to have clearer vision and see further and clearer.

As you begin to transition away from using your "I-sight" into using your 20/20 Character Vision, you begin to see people's hearts and understand hearts cannot lie. I believe most women filter the world through their hearts, while men filter the world through their eyes. If true, it is no wonder women are known to have "intuition" and a "sixth sense." They are merely using their 20/20 Character Vision.

In Mark chapter 8, the man Jesus ultimately healed started off not seeing, then he went to seeing people as trees.

In essence, Jesus became an Optometrist and helped the man to see.

> *Once again Jesus placed His hands on the man's eyes,*
> *and when he opened them his sight was restored*
> *and he could see everything clearly...* (Mark 8:25).

This man took a trip to see the Great Eye Doctor! He saw the Heavenly Optometrist who restored his sight.

Many of us should ask God to touch our sight so that we can see the world and people around us more clearly. We need to see people, to see women, to see our children for who they really are in their hearts.

Once the man had his sight restored and was able to see clearly, Jesus did not just go on his way. Jesus did not just say, "Okay, see ya." Jesus admonished the man. Jesus told him, "not to go back into that village." In other words, once you can see things clearly, do not go back. Do not allow yourself to be caught up in seeing things the way you once did. Do not allow yourself to go from using 20/20 Character Vision to using "I-sight" again.

When you think about your failed relationships, one of the most common things that will come to your mind is how often you used "I-sight" instead of character vision. You know you have been look-ing at people, women particularly, and perhaps your wife or ex-wife specifically, in the wrong way. You know you have been looking at their outward appearance, their persona and their facade. Now it is time to look beyond those masks and illusions and begin to see what is real in them. It is time to see their heart. It is time you correct your vision.

Correct Your Vision for Your Children

Having corrected vision so you see substance and not form is just as important to your children as it is to you. If you do not operate with corrected vision you will not see your children's hearts, pain and character. It is seeing your children's true character that makes fighting for their happiness worth it!

Your daughter filters her life through your lenses. Your son imitates your behavior and ultimately becomes you or your antithesis. So, understanding this whole vision thing is critical to helping your children develop into the kind of people that will experience a rewarding, fulfilling life. Our children should benefit from our experiences, not suffer through them. As we go about our sometimes shallow and pedestrian lives, we must remember we have little eyes watching us and little hands and feet following our example. Aside from learning the value of substance over surface for our own happiness, we must learn it for the well-being of our children.

As I reflect back on my children and the journey on which I took them, there was a pivotal point where I began to wonder about my children's vision. I began to look at them with my third eye and began to study them to determine the effect my actions were having on their vision. I saw my son grow, mature and begin to process the entire world through his "I-sight." He started, as most young men do, to see the world according to himself and what he wanted. Unfortunately, my example, or lack thereof, was not positively influential on his view of life. Regrettably, at the time he was paying close attention to me, I was still using my "I-sight." I did not model the right vision a young man should possess. I started off just trying to maintain my sanity. I didn't want a war with my ex. Perhaps it was for the good of my children, but if I am honest, there was also something that had a lot to do with me not wanting collateral damage to my own life, much less that of my children.

I started off being selfish, listening to other guys tell me to hide my money and hiring a lawyer that specialized in making it difficult for wives to win in court. So, as my son looked at me, the only moral vision he could develop was "I-sight."

Through conversations and observation of my son's growth, God quickly opened my eyes and my heart and I began looking at my ex, my children and the world with 20/20 Character Vision. My son, as all young boys do, looked at me to determine the man he would or would not become. My example informed his definition of manhood. In some ways, that was a good thing. And, unfortunately, in a lot of other ways, I failed; therefore, it was a bad thing. But remember, failing is not the end of the story, it is the beginning. When you fail, you receive an opportunity to go back and do it again. You receive a "do over." So, when I got my chance at a do over, I prayed hard to God that my vision be corrected. I prayed hard that God would bless my son with better vision than I had.

When I enrolled into the Marine Corps, I wanted to fly jets. In order to do so, I had to take a battery of tests, to include a fairly exhaustive eye vision test. After completing the test, I was told I had 20/10 vision. Wow, if only I could have 20/10 Character Vision. That would be awesome. In that case, I could be an example to my son and a role model to my daughter.

I saw my daughter turn inward and focus likes a laser on herself. I saw her use blurry-eyed vision to view herself. I saw her allow others to be her eyes. Unfortunately, my beautiful daughter was convinced by others that she failed the character test, as well as the "I-sight" test. They convinced her she was ugly inside and out. Again, I was so tied up into my own "I-sight," I did not notice her swerving over the road because her vision was impaired. I was so blinded by my own vision issues I did not notice my daughter's vision had been severely and significantly compromised. The truth is it was my son's "I-sight" and my daughter's compromised vision that convinced me to write this book.

I know I did not do things right. I was not the perfect divorced Dad. The need to stay committed to being a Dad, even after the divorce is a strong source of continued responsibility. I have banged up knees and scraped up elbows as a result of the mental and social limitations of my poor life vision. I am determined these injuries will benefit someone looking for a better future. I have fallen many times. But for the sake of my children, I got back up and tried again. I was troubled by a compounded sense of regret and failure, but the Great Optometrist restored my sight and told me not to go back to that "I-sight" village ever again. The next step is establishing my new Dads of Faith ministry to make sure others stay away from the village of hopelessness and regret.

You may be devastated by divorce because of bad character traits displayed by either you or your ex, but that does not give you the right not to live up to the expectations of your children. You must be realistic, and place your own expectations in a more responsible frame of mind in order to do for your children what you failed to do for yourself.

CHAPTER 4

UNNECESSARY WAR

Divorce is often an unnecessary war. Too often the divorce process ends with a range of emotions clustered together: anger, rage, jealousy, hurt, vengeance, slander, name calling and even vitriol. The very person we apparently loved so much we now loathe. But what about the children? It is impossible to understand what your children are feeling when they see their parents at one another's throat. Name calling. Bashing. Cursing. All for what? Who gets to keep the sofa or the dining room set?

Entering my divorce, I began to hoard items by creating a mental inventory:

This is mine.

"I bought this."

"So and so gave this to me."

"I am keeping this because she is not even into collecting these!"

So much of what became important was an issue of things.

I dug into my bunker. I prepared for war. I gathered my word bombs and opened my gun safes. My focus was on preserving my livelihood and my "stuff." It was not about my children. I was preparing for war. I became swept up in defense. I became obsessed with limiting what she got and protecting what I had. I did not want to be another divorced man who ended up living in a one room studio apartment, paying thousands to my ex, while she lived in a beautiful four-bedroom home. I refused to be sent to the poor farm, while she "maintained the standard of living to which she had become accustomed, while married to me."

I shuttered to even think of that.

There was something inherently unfair in my mind about it being more important that she maintain her standard, regardless of whether I did. I was totally focused on me. Barricaded in my bunker. Ready for war. Everyone told me this was what happens during a divorce and I was all about living out that stereotype.

When I stepped outside myself and looked down at Ken Gordon Jr. hunkered in "his" war bunker, I wondered:

"How in the world did I get here?"

"What brought me to this place?"

"What made it a war in the first place?"

"How did we get from I do to Oh no you won't?"

It started simply enough. Divergent paths. More time spent working for someone else than time spent working on us. Dimming of the "I-sight." Competing goals. The list goes on. In my case it was more of a difference of what we wanted in life. I do not begrudge my ex for what she wanted and I do not begrudge myself either. Did I want too much? Perhaps. Were my priorities right? Not really. Did we grow apart and in opposite directions? Yeah. Did I allow other things to interfere with my focus and my identity? Definitely.

Our slow slide down Divorce Hill began. We tried marital counseling even though I already made up my mind I was getting divorced. I was treading water. I was biding my time. I wanted to wait until my children got a little older. I wanted to wait until I was more financially secure so the divorce did not wipe me out. I worried about the impact on my credit. I worried about the impact on my job. I worried about the impact it would have in the community. I worried about the impact it would have on my reputation. I worried about what the kids in my children's school would say to, and about, them. I worried. Then I worried some more.

At that point a funny thing started happening. The more I worried, the more I needed someone to blame and it sure as heck was not going to be me.

Of course, I blamed my ex. She was my whipping post. She was my scapegoat. I took my anger, insecurity and fears out on her and it fueled an unnecessary war.

I worked myself into a tizzy obsessing about all the things that would and could go wrong. I worried about all the ways she and her lawyer would try to suck me dry. I believe this is typical. The shadow of the divorce is enough to fuel anger, paranoia and stress. So, the more we think about it, the greater the likelihood the final event will live up to our mental billing.

There were arguments, fighting, and anger. There was the onslaught of the five stages of grief. I first denied the inevitable. I thought could stay in my marriage for the sake of the children.

However, I was miserable and making her miserable too.

Then came the anger. The anger at her for not being able to work everything out, even though I was not helping. The anger at her for not being who I built her up to be in my mind. The anger at her for myriad illogical and nonsensical reasons. The anger at myself for getting into this predicament in the first place! The anger at myself for not getting out sooner. The anger at life. The anger at God. The anger at—just everything.

Next came the bargaining. Okay, so if I do this, then maybe this will happen. I can cut a deal and make this work. I can figure this out by doing "x." "If only," I said. "If only I would have…" "If only she would have." Then came the guilt and the backward looks.

Beyond that ticket to nowhere, came the depression. Empty feelings. I wanted to withdraw from life. At times I wanted to withdraw from married life and throw myself headfirst into single life. I wanted to blunt the feelings with whatever would make me feel good. But on the inside, there was a fog of intense sadness. I wondered if there was any point in going on alone? Why go on at all? I looked at myself. I was older. Fatter. More out of shape. Less attractive. Who would want me? Who could love me? Those were feelings of depression and like quicksand; it was sucking me down fast.

However, an amazing thing happened. Time moved forward and healed my wounds. Finally, I was ready for the final stage, which was acceptance. This stage was not about being okay. It was about accepting the reality of my situation and recognizing I was looking at my new permanent reality. I was unsure I would appreciate my new norm, but I eventually accepted it. I learned to live with it. The divorce was going to happen and I was going to survive.

I had a choice to make. Who comes first? The very fact I was getting divorced indicated part of the decision was already made. Sure, I could have hung around, unhappy, miserable and constantly messing up. I could have done all the wrong things for all the right reasons—I could have stayed because of the children, but mistreated my wife, cheated on my wife, became emotionally unavailable, or wrapped myself in a cocoon of "I do not want to be here." Let me be very clear, I am not endorsing, encouraging or condoning divorce. I am not suggesting one should see it as an alternative to doing the necessary work to keep a marriage intact. The Bible discourages divorce. Divorce is mentioned several times in the Old and New Testament, as God hates divorce, and there are very few exceptions where divorce is allowed in Scripture.

> *Jesus answered, "Anyone who divorces his wife and marries another woman commits adultery against her. And if she divorces her husband and marries another man, she commits adultery"* (Mark 10:11–12).

> *"The man who hates and divorces his wife," says the Lord, the God of Israel, "does violence to the one he should protect," says the Lord Almighty. So be on your guard, and do not be unfaithful"* (Malachi 2:16).

The Word of God clearly says you are supposed to protect your wife, not divorce and hate her.

The Bible's few occasions for acceptable divorce were infidelity and "finding something unpleasing about her."

> *If a man marries a woman who becomes displeasing*
> *to him because he finds something indecent about her*
> *and he writes her a certificate of divorce gives it to*
> *her and sends her from his house…* (Deuteronomy
> 24:1–4)

When the Scripture speaks of "finding something indecent about her," it refers to acts that are permanent and not things such as "she needed a bath" or "she was on her monthly cycle." It refers to Spiritual uncleanness, for which God has no tolerance. It covers things such as being an idol worshipper or bringing shame or dishonor to God's Word. Either way, there is nothing within the Bible that condones frivolous divorce, irreconcilable differences, an unwillingness to work on a marriage, or "just being tired of being married."

Marriage is considered, "being joined together by God." That which is of God, no man can tear apart. But, that which is not of God will not stay together.

When we marry and get divorced, there is a Spiritual aspect that must be addressed. Forgiveness and repentance is necessary. God views marriage as honorable. Therefore, it follows that our carefree, lackadaisical attitude is an affront to God. However, even so, God clearly understood that it would happen. Thus, he provided specific parameters for its existence.

It is clear divorce will occur, even as it did in the Old and New Testaments. If it is inevitable and occurs, there is yet a responsibility the man has and that responsibility is towards the children and towards the woman he once took as his bride and promised to love and cherish. I know, I know, that can be hard to grasp, but I believe strongly a man's responsibility towards his children is to protect and provide, whether married or otherwise. A man's responsibility towards his children cannot be cancelled by a court order or a judge's gavel. A man's responsibility towards his children is truly until death do them part. A man's responsibility towards his children is more than just paying child support. It is not about just sending the check every month. The Bible outlines the responsibility of a man from the time of Adam. Our job is to work, to live by the sweat of our brow—to provide for women, who provide for our heirs.

We therefore have the responsibility of providing for our children and to a measurable extent even to our ex.

I am not saying you have to fully support her or treat her as if she is your wife for eternity. But I submit, as a man—a real man—there is a responsibility you have to the woman with whom you shared a bed and to whom birthed your children.

But, guys check this out; I am not saying your responsibility is purely financial. Certainly not. Your responsibility is to not fight unnecessary wars: financial, material, societal and custodial. One needs look no further than the example of Jesus, to find someone who refused to fight unnecessary wars.

Through the New Testament, the Pharisees accosted, confronted, and attempted to provoke Jesus. Jesus often avoided conflict. Sometimes it meant "easing on down the road," as he did in John 4:3, Mark 1:14, or Matthew 4:12. Sometimes it meant simply holding one's peace, as he did when confronted by Judas and the soldiers in John 18 or on the cross in Luke 23. In both cases, Jesus addressed violent confrontation with peace and love. When confronted by Judas and the soldiers, he was more concerned about those with him. He asked them to let the others go.

Imagine, if instead of fighting an unnecessary war, we ask to let our children go, so they are not harmed. Instead of all out retaliation, we put the needs of our children first, so we do not lose them. That is the essence of my message in Divorced, but still Dad. You must be committed to your children and understand your civil responsibility. That is to say, your obligation to your ex and the mother of your children is to act civil and to treat her with respect. It's not about what you feel, it is about what is right.

The post-separation, post-relationship war that ensues when you seek to go your separate way is often a part of an unnecessary war. This unnecessary war pits two important people, in the lives of your children, against one another. There is often no refuge or protection for your children when their mother goes on the offensive to punish you for your sins, or when you seek to punish your ex for not being the dream woman you created in your mind, or when you attempt to punish your ex for her indiscretions or shortcomings.

More often than not, these are zero-sum wars.

In these wars no one wins. One could argue that wars do not yield winners, rather lesser losers. This is the case here. Who wins in a divorce? The attorneys, of course. Who wins in a divorce? The forces of evil that seek to tear down families and undermine all God intended for you, your wife and your children. Who wins in divorce? Only those who do not deserve to win. Therefore, you have the control. You determine the outcome, as well as the course.

> *...Your desire shall he for your husband, and he shall rule over you* (Genesis 3:16).

> *Fathers, do not provoke your children to anger, but bring them up in the discipline and instruction of the Lord* (Ephesians 6:4).

> *But I want you to understand that the head of every man is Christ, the head of a wife is her husband, and the head of Christ is God.* (1 Corinthians 11:3)

> *Wives, submit to your own husbands, as to the Lord. For the husband is the head of the wife even as Christ is the head of the church, his body, and is himself its Savior. Now as the church submits to Christ, so also wives should submit in everything to their husbands. Husbands love your wives, as Christ loved the church and gave himself up for her, that he might sanctify her, having cleansed her by the washing of water with the word.* (Ephesians 5:22–23).

From these Scriptures, I submit that the man, the husband, the father, was ordained by God to lead his household to Christ and to lead them to salvation. I submit that a man has a greater role than just to be provider and protector. In his own house, he must also be priest. From God's clear instruction for a father to raise his children in the discipline and instruction of the Lord, to God's instruction for a husband to love his wife and sanctify her, the Bible is very clear on the leadership role given to a man with his family. Therefore, it is my deduction that the husband, father and man are the Spiritual leader of his house, as Christ is the Spiritual leader of the church.

Accordingly, as the Spiritual leader, it is up to the man, the Dad, to determine the course of the divorce. If you are emotional, the divorce will be emotional. If you are ambivalent, the divorce will be emotional. If you are petty, the divorce will be emotional. Do you see a pattern? However, if you are prayerful and kind, if you are fair and focused, or if you are not vengeful or hateful, then the divorce will be less traumatic.

So, this begs the question, "What if he (I can hear the voice of the ex or the children in my ear) were that way from the beginning!?"

"Wouldn't we have averted this?"

After my divorce from my children's mother, I ended up remarrying. At some point, my daughter, observing my treatment of my new wife, asked to speak to me. She told me if I would have treated her mother the way I treat my wife, maybe we would not have gotten a divorce. Her words were posed as much as a question, as it was a statement. Was this the case? If I would have just been nicer, less hateful and more prayerful, would that have prevented a divorce?

A question like that is far too complicated to sum up in a one-word answer. But if I had to answer, it would be—possibly.

The truth is, only you know if the marriage would have thrived had you changed. Only you know if the root of your problem was simply a change in attitude resulting in a change in course. However, regardless of the answer, the fact is we could spend our entire lives living in the world of "what if."

Frankly, that is one stage of grief. In the bargaining stage, we ask ourselves all the "what if" questions (notice it's a stage not a permanent place). Move quickly through this stage because you can never truly answer a "what if" question. All you can do is learn from it.

Perhaps if you would have been nicer, you would still be married. Perhaps if you would have prayed more, you would still be married. Perhaps if you would have been less hateful, you would still be married. Perhaps if you would have been more attentive, you would still be married. Or, perhaps not. So, the answer to this very complex question is, as "Mister" said in the Alice Walker movie, "The Color Purple," "Could be and could be not! Who's to say?"

As a Christian Counselor, I do not encourage those I counsel to get caught up in the "what ifs." If you are not yet divorced, then try it. Can't hurt. If you are divorced, learn from it and apply it to your next relationship. May help.

However, all that being said, I answered my daughter:

"Honey, while that seems so simple, the truth is your mother and I tried. We were just not able to make our marriage work. It was not because I was mean to her or because I did not pray. It was because we are better as friends than we were as husband and wife. That does not mean we do not love you and your brother. It is does not mean we do not care about one another. It just means we were not able to make our marriage work. However, we both love you and your brother and will be here for both of you, no matter what."

What your children want is the security of knowing you, Mr. Dad, are not going anywhere. They can handle the marriage not working if their Dad is still there for them, if it does not mean you will disappear and as long as they are absolutely certain you divorcing their mother does not mean you divorcing them.

No divorce is easy.

While some divorces go smoothly, result in little financial upheaval and allow an exit without huge financial burdens, every divorce takes a toll. The toll may not be easily and immediately recognizable. The toll may not manifest itself for many years. Nonetheless, to a child, the dissolution of their parent's marriage is never easy. Not when they are 8.

Not when they are 28. No one escapes divorce unscathed. However, your ability to avoid unnecessary wars and focus on what is best for your children's mental, psychological, social and relational development remains the most important goal.

At the very beginning of the process, you make a decision whether you will fight a war or negotiate a truce. You make a decision whether you will give your money to the attorneys or to your children. It is truly that simple. Once you make that determination and your actions follow your decision, you control the path forward. Every divorce does not have to be ugly. Because some people want to "take it there," does not mean you have to "go there."

Let her hurl boulders, throw daggers and attempt to emasculate you. Let her do what she will. You have no control over her, but you have control over you. And you determine how vicious and nasty the war will be. Nothing is more foolish than the sight of one person fighting while the other does nothing. Is it difficult? Yes. Is it tempting to "go there?" Yes. But, the question comes back to, "Are your children worth it?"

Somewhere in all of this, you must not fight unnecessary wars so you can give your children a healthy future, because your children are worth it!

The die has been cast and you're either out of the marriage or about to be out of the marriage, so you should salvage as much of your children's sanity, security and self-worth as you can.

You may not have been able to save the relationship with your children's mother, but you can absolutely save the relationship with your children.

Your children's mental and psychological health and wellbeing is worth you holding your peace and not striking out or retaliating. Their mental and psychological health is worth you not engaging in an unnecessary war. Just like working all those hours and sacrificing all the things you did was worth it to give your children a chance to attend that private school, or play on that athletic team or take those music lessons, so too is making the sacrifice of peace, at a time when going to war feels so right.

At that very moment when you are angry and your ex has asked for more money, or more stuff, think about what is important in your life and what will last.

Your job will not last.

Your car will not last.

Your house will not last.

Your country club membership will not last.

Your super fine, tight butt, perky breast sex toy who loves you so much, who listens to you when no one else will and who makes you feel so much younger, will not last either.

But your children and their children? That is what is important. That is what lasts. Your name living on, is what lasts. Yes, your children are worth it because they are how you live forever. Your children offer you life forever—as you live through them and their children. So, I ask you again, is holding your peace, not going on the offensive and being generous to your children's mother worth it?

Are your children worth it?

The unequivocal answer is absolutely.

If you are on the offensive, stop in your tracks and think of your children. If you are hunkered down in a bunker, ready to defend "all you have worked so hard for," then stop thinking of all the stuff you will lose and think about how much worse it would be to lose your children. If you are the one being nasty and vindictive, then think of how your terrible attitude, which is as much your fault as anyone's, is affecting your children and their entire future.

Remember, it was your "I-sight" and your lack of 20/20 Character Vision that contributed to you being where you are. It takes two to tango, so as much as you want to blame it all on your ex, you had culpability as well. So rage to the world. Yell and act a fool in court. But when you are alone, look at yourself and be honest. Man up. Then stop the foolishness and think about being a protector, provider and priest to your children.

If she is the one on the offensive, let her rage. If she is the one taking the war to you, let her go off. You think of your children.

For the sake of your children, do not allow yourself to be lured into war, if your children's mother is attempting to bait you. If you choose to go to war, it will be because you must, not because you were goaded. If you choose to go to war it will be because you needed to defend, not because you needed to inflict. Do not fight unnecessary wars, the present and future casualties can be catastrophic.

When I got divorced, I sat down with my wife, who was angry and injured, and I told her we could do it one of two ways. I told her we could do it the easy way, which was to take the money we would use for the attorneys and instead use it for the children. I told her if we do it this way, she had my word I would pay child support in a timely manner and would not fight doing so. I told her if we did it the easy way I would pay her enough alimony to ensure she always had a roof over the heads of my children.

Contrariwise, I told her if we did it the hard way, I would "lawyer up," as she had, and we would spend months and perhaps years in the courts, fighting over every little thing, exhausting both of our savings and checking accounts and in the end, our children would show the scars of the court battles and neither of us would be the better for it. Fortunately, for me, even though my wife was hurt and angry, she was still willing to be sensible.

I am a firm believer that most women just want us to do the right thing. They are not crazy. They understand when it is over. Truth is, many of them are relieved when it is over. Many of them are tired of cleaning up after us. Tired of being the cook and the maid. Tired of being the on demand sex provider. Tired of picking up our dirty socks and underwear off the floor. Tired of wondering where you are and who you are doing. Oh, trust me, Mr. Man! As much as you think you are such a catch and she will be devastated at your departure, I can assure you her negative reactions are not always about her losing her "Boo" or her "Bae." Many times her negative reactions are about how she is treated on the way out the door.

When the divorce comes, women want to be treated kindly and regarded highly for their contributions to the marriage. Women want to be honored for giving children to the marriage. Women want to be respected for sacrificing their careers and, in some cases, their personal dreams, on behalf of having a family. No woman wants to be "paid" for what they did. They do not think a dollar figure can be placed on bringing life into the world, keeping the household running smoothly, or sacrificing their career, dreams and hopes so their husband could thrive. Women just want to be respected and expect us to do right by them.

Admittedly, therein lies the rub. What one person feels like is "doing right by them" and what another person feels, can be worlds apart. However, that is where calm, sensible communication comes into the picture. That is when putting first things first, i.e. your children, comes into the picture. For the sake of my children, I was willing to be generous and accommodating. Out of respect for her bearing my two wonderful children, I was willing to do a little more. In recognition for the sacrifices she made for me,

I was willing to go above and beyond what others felt I should.

Let others opine. Only you know how important your children and their future are to you. Let others say whatever they want, only you and your children's mother know how much she truly sacrificed to establish and care for your family. Give her the security of knowing you remember and will never forget.

> *God is not unrighteous to forget your work and labor of lovey which you have showed toward his name...* (Hebrews 6:10).

God expects us to do as he does, not just as he says. If God will not forget someone's work and labor of love, then we are challenged, as those who say we love God, to do the same.

Give your children's mother the security of knowing you will not forget the work she did for your household, your children, and your family. Something about showing kindness and providing security makes women sensible and willing to put down their weapons and work collaboratively on what is best for both of you and your children.

Commit you will not be the one to go to war. Commit you will not be the one to go on the offensive or the defensive. Commit, for the good of your children, you will be honorable and respectful. Commit you will keep both of you out of court and off the lawyer's accounts receivable ledgers by paying what you generously agreed upon. Stop thinking about how it benefits her and think about how it benefits your children. Stop worrying about what she is doing with the money and think about honoring her work and labor of love.

I gave my children's mother my word I would pay child support and alimony in a timely manner, would not fall behind and would communicate exactly what was going on with me financially if she was willing to call off the war and instead focus on how we proceed in peace.

Do not fight unnecessary wars.

Commit you will do whatever it takes to convince your soon-to-be ex-wife, or your ex, to put down the howitzers and instead work with you to make the most out of a bad situation—for the sake of your children.

CHAPTER 5

BE A MAN

Know your responsibilities as a man. Merriam–Webster's Learner's Dictionary defines a man as one possessing a high degree of the traits considered distinctive of manhood. According to the Psychology of Men by Dr. Will Meek, the following traits are representative of manhood: emotional toughness, courage, self-reliance, rationality, duty, loyalty, responsibility, integrity, selflessness, compassion, competitiveness, ambition, and risk-taking.

If you were a fly on the wall when I would speak to my son during his early teen years, you would have heard me tell him being a man is about taking responsibility, not blaming others, working hard, leading by example, protecting your family, and providing for your family. Despite sharing those traits with him, I tried not to make it complex. I didn't want to overload him with information. I made it very simple.

"Being a man is about taking responsibility," I told him.

Real men embrace their responsibility. They do not run from it. Every other trait addressed by Dr. Meek is an outgrowth of responsibility.

When you stand at an altar and say, "I do," you are accepting responsibility. When you bring children into the world, you are accepting responsibility. While a court order can alleviate you of your duty toward a wife, there is no court, law, or entity that can relieve you of your responsibility towards your children.

As a man, you have a responsibility to care for your children and you shouldn't rely on another man to care for them.

The "Another Man" Predicament

Second marriages involving children are an unavoidable reality. As a result, parents find themselves in a position where their children have another parent in their lives.

Jealousy, territorialism and paranoia may set in.

"I do not want you calling another man dad."

"I am your only father!"

These thoughts and feelings create confusion and additional problems for your children. Do you honestly think they will forget you are their father? If you have been their provider, protector and priest, do you really think your children will try to replace you?

I've always known children love unconditionally. No matter what, a child never forgets their parent. Others may do things for them. Others may help them. But they know there's always dad!

Insecurity is the problem and your issue alone.

If your ex's new mate is not mean, abusive or indifferent to your children and, if he desires a relationship with your children and is willing to put in the requisite time, you should thank God. Focus on the positive. Now your children have two men who care for them in their lives.

Yes, your mind can certainly go crazy imagining the "what ifs?"

...he mistreats them?

...he is a child molester?

...he turns them against me?

...he is a better father than me?

...they respect him more than me?

"What if they love him more than they love me!?"

[Sound of screeching brakes]

That is what this is really all about. You are concerned your children will love someone else more than you. Do not be insecure. If you are not the father you should be—a provider, protector, priest—

it's not too late. Do not confuse your children by giving them ultimatums, hard choices or petty dictates like, "you better not call him dad." Instead, step up to the plate and be a great dad. And if your children are lucky and blessed, they will have two great men in their lives that care for them.

Another man can augment the care of your children and contribute to the care of your children and if that happens it's a bonus for your children. But your children are your responsibility. You dictated as much when you laid down with their mother. The worst thing in the world is to have a male impregnate a female, then walk away from his responsibility. Remember, getting someone pregnant does not make you a dad. Getting someone pregnant makes you a sperm donor! A dad is a man. A man accepts full responsibility for his actions, his words, and his deeds. I implore you to be a man.

What does it mean to provide, protect and be a priest?

By the sweat of your brow you will eat your food
until you return to the ground (Genesis 3:19).

Matthew's Commentary explains the Scripture as, "His employments and enjoyments are embittered to him. Labour is his duty, which he must faithfully perform; it is part of man's sentence, which idleness daringly defies." So, it is our plight to work. We work to provide for our families. We work to ensure they have a comfortable life. That's what men do; we work. Whether it is one job or three jobs, we do what we have to in order to take care of our household. Prior to my divorce, I embarked upon an entrepreneurial venture that went bad. As a result, I was left with bills and responsibilities, but no job. So guess what I did?

Did I find a sugar mama to give me money?

Did I go to my parents asking for money?

Did I move my family back to my parent's house?

Did I get on welfare?

None of the above.

I went out and got three jobs. I worked during the day selling cars. I worked in the evening as a garbage man. And, I worked two twelve hour shifts on the weekend at a hotel. I did whatever I needed to do to provide for my family.

That is what a man does.

A man should not put his wife in a position to get a job to provide for the family. He shouldn't pout or complain if she doesn't want to get a job, he should do whatever it takes, including, getting another job. And while women should have a willingness to assist in the household, especially if she has the skills and is comfortable working, she should want to get a job. Marriage is a partnership requiring husband and wife to contribute, albeit in different ways.

Nonetheless, I have never mandated my wife get a job. I have always been okay with her making the choice. Sometimes she worked outside of the house. Sometimes she chose to work inside the house. Either way, I was prepared and did whatever I needed to do regardless of her decision. Whatever you choose to do, do it and do not live above your means, as a man is also a good steward. If you are spending twice what you are bringing in and aren't willing to get more jobs, then you are behaving as a child. Sorry, but that's the truth.

Provider, Protector, and Priest

A man works.

He works hard and as much as necessary to take good care of his family. Notice I said good care. Working at a minimum wage job and saying it is all you can do, if you have a family, is not sufficient. Work three minimum wage jobs if you have to. A man is never lazy. It is an affront to your moral responsibility.

A man is a protector.

1 Peter 3:7 refers to the woman as the "weaker" vessel. Let me be clear. This is not talking about mentally or psychologically. While some strut about thinking it is more of a physical statement, the truth is in some cases that is not at all accurate either. The statement is not absolute and is in no way a reflection on the value or strength of women. I like Dr. Eddie I. Hyatt's editorial interpretation of this passage, which was published on April 15, 2015 in Charisma News.

In the passage he says,

> *"A careful examination of this passage will reveal that Peter is not referring to a weaker frame or constitution of the woman, but to a weaker status in the culture of the day. A closer look will also reveal that Peter is not affirming a male hierarchy in marriage but is calling for mutual respect and partnership."*

Based on this interpretation, and that of other theologians, it is clear there is an imbalance in the cultural receptivity and status of women. So, it is up to men to demand mutual respect and treatment of women. It is up to men to fight against injustice. To regard women as weaker, less employable or less talented is to promulgate intolerance and ignorance. It is the responsibility of those who are not subjected to discrimination to advocate and fight for those who are. As Dr. Martin Luther King, Jr. famously wrote in his Letter from the Birmingham Jail, "Injustice anywhere is a threat to justice everywhere." So a man must be a protector of his helpmeet and his household.

A man must be a priest to his household.

A man's role is to lead his family in the worship of God. Men want to be the head in so many different areas, but quickly cede the responsibility to others when it comes to faith. Here is my thing: If you find out your children are not going to church, do not believe in God, are confused about who to call on in the time of trouble, then blame no one but yourself if you did not lead them to God and show them how to pray and how to worship. Enough said.

The essence of a man is to love and to honor. How does a man love and honor his children? Through deed, action and word. He tells them he loves them regularly, out loud and publicly. He hugs and kisses them. Yes, even the boys. Boys need to know it is okay for a father to hug his son. Boys need to know it is okay for a father to kiss them on the cheek. There is nothing wrong with a dad showing affection towards his children. As a matter of a fact, there is something wrong if he does not.

A man shows love by staying in his children's lives in positive ways, even after divorce. A man shows love and honor when he seeks to know his children's pain. A man shows love and honor when he listens to his children and shows respect for their input and insight.

The essence of a man is to show strength and control. Demonstrating restraint to his children, before, during, and after divorce proceedings. An ability to control his emotions, impulses and actions. No matter how upset he may become, a man understands he must always model to his children that discipline and restraint are invaluable and indispensable traits. It is easy to be the one cursing and yelling. Sure you can "go there." It is easy to be the one who goes off and "tells someone about themselves." Doing those things will teach your children nothing and may even cause them to lose respect for you, especially if you do those things to their mother.

Provide, protect, love, honor, show strength and demonstrate control. These are qualities God intended man to possess from the beginning of creation. This is illustrated from the very first family in the Bible. Adam's job was to protect the earth and the woman God created from him. He created Eve from Adam's rib because he wanted Eve's place to be at Adam's side. He did not create Eve from a bone in Adam's foot, as she was not supposed to be beneath him. He did not create Eve from a bone from Adam's skull, as she was not supposed to be above him. He did not create Eve from a bone in Adam's back, as she was not supposed to be behind him. He did not create Eve from a bone in Adam's front as she was not supposed to shield him. Rather, he created Eve from a bone on Adam's side, as she was supposed to be the most comfortable when she was at his side.

Adam's role was that of caretaker. He was to be caretaker of the earth and all that was within, which included Eve. Adam's role was to have dominion over all things and to show forth the glory of God through obedience to, and fellowship with, his maker and Lord.

However, based on his recalcitrant actions we were doomed from the beginning by the first man—Adam. Generally, Eve is the one blamed for the failings of the Earth's first couple. She was the one who heard God say "do not eat the fruit," yet she spoke to and was beguiled by the snake. It is so easy to blame Eve and focus on all she did to cause the fall. And yes, I would agree there was a commission of a great sin, but not the way some see it.

The great sin was not Eve being beguiled by the serpent. The great sin was not Eve eating the fruit or even her giving it to Adam. No, before that ever occurred, in my opinion, sin had already been committed. How so? It was committed when Adam lost touch with Eve.

God gave man dominion over the birds of the air, the fish of the sea and the animals of the earth. He gave all things to be subject to and controlled by Adam.

> *So God created man in his own image, in the image of God created he him; male and female created he them. And God blessed them, and God said unto them, Be fruitful and multiply, and replenish the earthy and subdue it [bring under control]; and have dominion over the fish of the sea and over the fowl of the airy and over every living thing that moveth upon the earth* (Genesis 1:27–28).

He took the man and put him into the Garden of Eden to dress it and to keep it. So, it is clear from this Biblical text that part of man's role and privilege was having control of the earth and dominion over all upon the earth.

Yet, the very person who was bone of his bone and flesh of his flesh, with that person he lost touch.

> *And the man [Adam] said, The woman whom thou gavest to be with me, she gave me of the tree, and I did eat* (Genesis 3:12).

So herein are a number of firsts. This is the first time a man deflects his responsibilities onto a woman. Dude, it was your job to make sure your family did according to the Word of God!

Do not blame your helpmeet!

This is the first time we see a man blaming someone other than himself. This is the first time we see a man not "manning up" and having honor. I have no Biblical verse or text for my next statement, all I have is my belief. The reason Adam was punished was because of not living up to being a man. He was created in the image of God. He was not created in the image of a slithering, whining, complaining, blame shifting low-life. He was supposed to be a stand up person. He was supposed to keep his house in order. He was supposed to be a man through thick and thin. Whether the woman did what she was supposed to do or not. Whether the woman abided by the vows or not. Whether the woman was somewhere talking to a snake or not. HE was the MAN and it was his responsibility to be the man, no matter what. He was given dominion over all things and it was his job to preside over, supervise and lead, not only all the animals, but over his woman, as well.

So, you say, "Yeah, right. You try to control a woman and see where that gets you… " and trust me, I will not argue that point. However, one must think what would have happened if Adam would not have taken his position so lightly. What would have happened if Adam would have sought to have dominion over Eve, as he had over the animals?

What would have happened if Adam would have been diligent to the needs of his woman—instructing her, providing companionship, providing direction?

> *And when the woman saw that the tree was good for*
> *food and that it was pleasant to the eyes, and a tree*
> *to be desired to make one wise, she took of the fruit*
> *thereof and did eat* (Genesis 3:6).

God endowed Adam with dominion over all the earth, with the responsibility to be a provider and with the job of naming all the animals. Why did Eve need to look for food and wisdom? Clearly, God had already provided all of that. Eve was off looking for something they already possessed.

She was off shopping for shoes, when her closet was already chock full of Jimmy Choos, Manolo Blahniks, Christian Louboutins, Miu Mius, and Walter Steigers. Part of being a man is about a heaping of effective communication, with a generous dash of mutual understanding. It is a man's responsibility to ensure his household is on the same page, fully informed and in complete understanding, not only of his role, but also confident in his commitment to fulfill his role.

If Adam would have been a helpmeet to his helpmeet, would she have even struck up a conversation with the serpent? What if Adam's lack of control over Eve ushered in the original sin and ushered in the challenges we face to this day in "controlling and having dominion over women?"

In the natural order of things, everything and everyone answers to someone. As a matter of a fact, the very definition of dominion, according to Merriam-Webster's is to exercise a directing or restraining influence over. That is to say, according to the Biblical establishment of power, man and woman had dominion and influence over all things on the earth, with the woman being influenced by the man, as long as he was following the precepts of Christ.

> *But I want you to realize that the head of every man is Christy and the head of the woman is many and the head of Christ is God* (1 Corinthians 11:3).

So, it is already Biblically ordained that man is the head of woman. The issue is "how" one exerts that dominion or "headship."

A man does not lord over a woman. A man does not abuse this position of authority. A man understands he must lead and he must honor. A man is secure enough in himself that he does not need to make someone small so he can be big. A man does not need to "win." A man does not look at his wife like a conquest. A man understands the gravity of his role and responsibility. A man is a provider and a protector, period! Neither divorce, nor sickness, nor even death should stop a man from being a provider and a protector!

A male who abdicates his responsibility as a provider or protector as a result of a divorce was never a man. He was merely a male. The difference between being a male and being a man is that a man accepts and embraces his responsibility, no matter what, through thick and thin. A man ensures his children are provided for and protected, even post-divorce and he does so without concern that those provisions and protections may extend to the mother of his children. This fact does not obfuscate the issue. It is irrelevant. What's more, it should be accepted, if for no other reason that because she bore him his heirs.

After I was divorced, I did not lessen my support for my children, I stepped it up. So great was my desire to provide and protect for my children after my divorce that I gave sacrificially to their development and needs. I made a significant investment renovating the home where my children would live, post-divorce. I bought a home three blocks away in order to be close to my children. I reduced the amount of travel on my job in an effort to be present for my children. I agreed to more in child support and alimony to ensure my children had, even if I did not. I paid for clothes, uniforms, beauty and barber shop trips and other things for my children, on top of paying Child Support, because I wanted to ensure I did not punish my children or give them the impression they lost me. Whatever I could do for my children and whatever I could give them, I did so. I gave until it hurt. Why? Because they are my children. They did not choose to be in the situation they found themselves. It was my actions that put them there.

Excuse me, what was that you mumbled? It takes two to tango? I didn't do it by myself? If that is what you thought, then let me shout back to you to stand up and be a man.

You are the one endowed and appointed by God to lead. One who seeks to place blame on others is not one fit to lead. So, take responsibility for the fact that you are the leader. You are the man. Own it. They are your children. Your heirs. Their mother did the hard work of getting them here, while all you did was the easy (and fun) work of getting her pregnant.

So own your role and step into your responsibility. You are the male, so be the man. The woman is singularly responsible for childbirth. The woman manages the home. The woman is your helpmeet. She cannot birth if you do not plant. She cannot manage the home if you do not provide one. She cannot help if you do not work. A man loves, honors, provides and protects.

Like the Geico commercial says, "It's what we do."

CHAPTER 6

EMOTIONS

Divorce produces raw emotions. Anger, guilt, resentment, frustration, confusion, depression, feelings of betrayal, feelings of abandonment, and so many more. Some days you want to scream and others you want to cry. No matter how toxic, abusive or unfulfilling the marriage, when it is over you are awash in emotion. Being engulfed in emotions makes the divorce vitriolic, protracted and unrestrained. Even the most stoic and mentally unavailable person struggles with raw emotions during and after a divorce.

The end of a marriage is an emotionally painful experience. Thinking about the experience of divorce within the context of attachment generates a greater sense of empathy for what you might be feeling. It explains the levels of rage, vindictiveness, grief, and despair that so often accompany this common life transition. We too often think of divorce as a noun or a verb, but it is actually a relational trauma that has a physiological and emotional effect. You may be creating more suffering for yourself by resisting what you are feeling or telling yourself that you are overreacting.

Recognize that the end of your marriage represents much more for you than you may realize. If you were a small child and the person you depended on most was suddenly unavailable to you, there is no doubt you would have a strong reaction. The end of your marriage is no different. Give yourself the time and space to heal and repair. You are not damaged, just temporarily devastated, and the recovery will come with time. Divorce is not just a matter of the heart but an experience that impacts the whole person on a multitude of levels.

How are you as a man required to handle this deluge of emotions? Hey, remember, men aren't supposed to cry or feel emotion. We are rocks. We are the strong ones. Yes, all of that is true, but we are also human, flesh and blood. If you pinch us we jump, if you cut us we bleed (though everyone doesn't bleed black and gold, as do I and the brothers of my beloved fraternity – "06") men are human and not robots, so emotions are okay.

But, it is not acceptable for you to allow your emotions to control you.

How much is too much and where do you draw the line? From a counseling perspective, you must give yourself license to hurt.

You must give yourself permission to feel the pain, to allow it to engulf you and permeate your every cell. You must recognize it. You must accept it. You must embrace it. You must understand it. And then you must control it.

There are a number of ways to accomplish this. However, the best way begins with seeking help and assistance from a third party. Yes, you can grit your teeth and gut it out on your own. You can be your own therapist. However, let me know how that works out for you. Too many times people attempt to self-diagnose, self-counsel or self-medicate. The results are never good. While they "think" they have overcome or healed, they are often much worse than they were before.

In order to effectively advance through the healing process, one should enlist the assistance of a coach. Think of it like a rehab professional for your heart. After injuring yourself or after surgery, your doctor often prescribes Physical Therapy. Your doctor knows if you are entrusted to go home and put yourself through the paces of therapy, it will be incomplete and lacking. You will stop when you get tired. You will stop when it hurts. You will not start when you are not up to it.

So too is your plight if you attempt to self-administer your Mental Therapy.

If you are truly to recognize, accept and understand your emotions and what you must do in order to move forward, you will need an emotional coach, of sorts. You will need a Mental Therapist. Whether this person is a Christian Counselor or a professional therapist, is up to you. Just make sure you get a third party emotional coach to help navigate your path to healing and recovery. Through recognizing, accepting and understanding your emotional pain, you learn how to control it.

Like most things in our lives, the first step to controlling it is admitting it exists. You must "see" it first, before you can get your arms around it. You must understand the essence of it before you can hope to control it. You must bifurcate it before you can dissect it. There is good emotion and there is bad emotion. Just because you are hurting and your most prominent emotions are raw, does not mean emotion is a bad thing.

Actually, emotion is a good thing. It lets you know you are alive and connected. It lets you know you are human and reminds you of your vulnerabilities.

As a Christian Counselor, I encourage all I counsel not to run from emotion, but embrace it. Embrace it in a way that says, I know who you are. I feel your presence. But I am the one in control.

I once did a session where I had to address some hurtful truths with someone so they could get out of denial and deal with their deficiencies. I handed the person a stress ball and told her after I shared the feedback with her, she could throw the ball until she worked out her emotion. By working out her emotion, she could control it, as opposed to it controlling her. Once I shared my expert evaluation and assessments, I encouraged her to throw the ball. She threw it alright. Right at me. I handed it back to her and she threw it at me again. I handed it back to her and she threw it at me again. I allowed her to throw it at me again and again (did I mention she threw it at my face?) until she had it out of her system. At that point, she was ready to control the emotion and pursue a positive course towards addressing her issues. This too is the case with divorce emotions. Therefore, allow me to suggest a couple Emotion Control Tips (ECTs):

Emotional Control Tip #1: Grab a pillow that has a handle, get a sofa pillow or stand in front of a punching bag. Do this by yourself so no one will hear what you are about to say. Stop for a moment and think of all the reasons you are angry, guilty, demoralized, frustrated or resentful over the divorce.

When you think of a reason, shout it out;

Each time you shout out a reason hit the bed with the handled pillow, punch the punching bag or throw the sofa pillow at an empty wall:

How dare she! [punch]

After all I did for her [hit]

As hard as I worked and she has the nerve to [throw]

It was only a fling [punch]

It was just one night [hit]

How could she after I have been so faithful to her [throw] Why isn't she the person I need [punch]

Why did she let herself go [hit]

Why did she change so much [throw]

Take a moment. Breathe. Exhale deeply. Inhale deeply. Exhale deeply. Inhale deeply. Exhale deeply. Inhale deeply. Your goal is to do this breathing exercise three times before proceeding.

Do it again after shouting out another reason.

Repeat until you run out of reasons.

I am not here to judge the reasons for the divorce; I am just here to help you work it out of your system so you control it and not vice versa. Do this every night if you must. Do if for one or two weeks straight if you must. Just get it out. Another method is the "Dummy in the Chair" method.

Emotional Control Tip #2: Take a suit, article of clothing, pillow or some inanimate object and put it in a chair. If you have something that belonged to the subject person, all the better. Say everything you want to or need to, to that a person.

Get it all out.

Hold nothing back.

Yell at the person.

Cry in front of the person.

After you have finished and have nothing left to say, take the object, put it in a garbage bag and throw the bag in the garbage.

This symbolic gesture allows you to gain closure. It is often better to do this to an inanimate object than with the person themselves. Why? Well aside from it being illegal to stuff someone into a garbage bag and put them out on the curb, no matter how good our emotions tell us it would feel, it is because what is said, cannot be unsaid. Additionally, when we speak to an inanimate object, they cannot speak back and remind us of what we did (oops).

Nonetheless, embrace your emotions. Truly embrace them. Hold them. Control them. Do not let them control you. Emotions remind us we are alive. Allowing them to control us, sometimes makes us wish we were dead.

After my divorce, I was full of raw emotion. I felt angry, indignant, lonely, hurt, depressed, empty, guilty, and anxious. There were many days I wanted to scream and yell at my ex. There were many nights I wanted to cry and feel sorry for myself. As a counselor, it is often most difficult for us to ingest our own medicine. Recognizing this, I sought the assistance of a therapist. During sessions with my therapist, we utilized Emotion Control Tip #2. In addition to doing it during my therapy, I also did it at home.

I went to the store and bought a stuffed animal to represent my ex. And when I was feeling emotional, I would set it on my counter or in a chair in my room and unleash on it. It just sat there. Never said a word, although a couple times I am sure I saw it cringe and other times I am sure it looked as if I hurt its feelings. But, I used this inanimate object in the form of something I related to my ex to help me through the temporary uber-emotional period, in which I found myself.

And guess what? When I would see my ex, I was not compelled to say any hurtful, mean, incendiary things to her, because I had gotten them out of my system.

Will that work for you? I do not know. What works for one person may not work for another. In therapy, we keep trying things until we find something that works. Sometimes it is the most unremarkable thing that works for someone. Nothing fancy. Nothing complex. Sometimes, something that is very simplistic, but creates emotional stimulation and healing, is most effective.

The key is you have to be open to trying and continuing to try until you find whatever it is that works for you. You cannot try one or two things and when they do not work, disavow therapy. You cannot try one therapist and when you do not see immediate progress, disavow therapy and go it alone.

Understanding and controlling your emotions is one of the most important healing processes in your journey back to mental and psychological health and well-being after divorce.

Your goal is to be a Dad to your children, and you cannot effectively be a Dad if your emotions are controlling you. You must understand and control your emotions, which allows you to be mentally present and prepared to always be Dad.

CHAPTER 7

YOUR RELATIONSHIP WITH YOUR CHILDREN

The Bible is the ultimate how-to guide. This is the case even as it relates to our relationships with our children. God encourages us to be a teacher and an instructor to our children.

> *And these words that I command you today shall be on your heart. You shall teach them diligently to your children, and shall talk of them when you sit in your house, and when you walk by the way, and when you lie down, and when you rise* (Deuteronomy 6:6–7).

> *Tell your sons about it, And let your sons tell their sons, And their sons the next generation* (Joel 1:3).

Our role is one of preparing our children for the world, ensuring they know God, making sure they have a Spiritual foundation and assuring they understand His greatness.

> *We will not conceal them from their children, but tell to the generation to come the praises of the Lord,*

*And His strength and His wondrous works that He
has done* (Psalm 78:4).

*Train up a child in the way he should go and when
he is old he will not depart from it* (Proverbs 22:6).

We must train up our children, rear them, and raise them to
know and understand God and his purpose for them.

When it comes to the relationship with your children, you must
understand the gravity of your responsibility to them.

You must provide for your children and cannot afford to be
sidetracked or distracted from this primary responsibility. This
responsibility survives divorce or separation. As long as they are your
children, and they will be as long as you live, then you have a Biblical
responsibility to them!

*But if anyone does not provide for his own, and espe-
cially for those of his household, he has denied the faith
and is worse than an unbeliever* (1 Timothy 5:8).

In the course of divorce, we get distracted with the back and
forth of divorce positioning, the one-ups-man ship and the maneu-
vering inherent in divorce proceedings.

Trust me, I get it. Been there, done that.

When my ex and I separated, an immediate battle began over
"stuff." Who would get the art collection? Who would get the wine
collection? Who would get the barbeque grill? We started mentally
putting sticky notes on all our "stuff." "This is mine, and this is mine."

"I want this."

It was all about "stuff."

Stuff, by the way that you cannot take with you when you die.
Stuff that will not last. Stuff that can be replaced.

Then after all the fighting over "stuff" was over, we turned our
focus to our children. Who would get them? I wanted my children.
I thought long and hard about fighting for full custody. I thought
about what it would take to convince a judge I should have them

instead of my ex. The reality was if I was going to get them, I would have to convince the judge my ex was a pretty terrible person. I would have to lie through my teeth and throw buckets of mud and dirt on the mother of my children. While that may have achieved my desired outcome, I thought about the effect a selfish act like that would have on my children.

According to an article in "Pediatrics," Vol. 104-No. 1, July 1999, written by Jerome Kagan, PhD:

"The importance of identification for personality development means that the parent's personality, talents and character, as they are perceived by the child, are of significance." So children identify themselves based on how they perceive their parents. Children identify so closely with their parents that criticism about a parent is experienced as criticism of themselves. "

Given this fact, if you do everything you can to tear apart the mother of your children, then you are, in fact, tearing apart your children. If your attitude in gaining "stuff" or getting custody of your children is "by any means necessary," even if it means slander and subterfuge, then while you may get what you want and while you may do damage to the "hated" ex, I submit you are doing more damage to your children, their identity, their psyche, their self-esteem and their character.

So if your goal is to take part in raising your children, as the Bible instructs you to do in Proverbs 22:6 by requiring us to "train up a child in the way they should go," you cannot build them up and at the same time tear them down. Your total focus, especially post-divorce should be to build your children up!

> *So then we pursue the things which make for peace and the building up of one another* (Romans 14:19).

Our goal, post-divorce should be to make for peace, so we can focus on building up our children.

While I know from personal experience how difficult it can be to stay focused on doing the right thing on behalf of your children,

I will tell you from my own failings, that to do anything different can have catastrophic results. My children spent time in therapy after being subjected to hearing words of anger directed at and about their mother. No child should ever hear terrible things said about either of their parents. Moreover, they should never hear it from the other parent!

Casualty of War?

During the divorce, often a casualty of war becomes the relationship between the children and their dad. Most psychologists agree that a father is important for the child's development to instill discipline and other social skills. However, research evaluating children of divorce showed a more positive relationship with mothers than with fathers. In fact, research suggests the relationship with the father is often endangered (Van Schaick & Stolberg, 2001).

Children of divorce also reported less attachment to their fathers and rated them as less caring (Tayler, Parker & Roy, 1995). This can be expected when one considers that 85% of divorce cases end with physical custody of children being awarded to the mother (Maccoby & Mnookin, 1992).

There are several reasons for these perceptions and realities. First, if the mother is the one who spent the most time with the children during the marriage there is a greater bond and a more positive relationship with the mother. In these cases, the mother is home more often, helps the children with their homework, takes them to their games and generally interacts with them more. Therefore there is greater familiarity. While the children still recognize the father as their father, they simply have greater interaction with the mother, which often creates stronger bonds. Another way this can occur is if the children perceive the mother as the weaker of the two, therefore, associate her as being the victim. This is especially the case if the father commits infidelity. Children often take the side of the perceived victim in the break up.

When I was married to my ex, I was the strong man in the house. I was the disciplinarian. I was the one with the white- collar career. I was the one with the advanced education. I was the one with the political and community involvements. I was seen as strong and indestructible to my children, as are many men. This was great while I was married, but worked to my detriment when I got divorced.

After the divorce, my children expected me to "take it easy on their mother." As the divorce played out, I pursued "stuff," had my own lawyer and tried to protect myself from ending up in the poor-house. However, my children perceived it as me being a bully. They saw me as the bad guy and their mother as the victim. They did not ask my side of the story. They did not want to know my feelings or pain.

My children saw me as the big, indestructible, strong man fighting against a small, helpless woman, who was their mother. Their mother, who was always there for them, who helped them with their homework, who cooked all their meals, and who washed all their clothes, was the victim. It did not matter what she did or did not do. It did not matter whose fault it was. Nothing mattered except I was being a bully and at the end of the day, it was my fault. Period. No explanation needed thank you. They felt they could see which of us was outwardly affected more and because that someone was not me, they opined it must have been my fault.

As a result of perceptions and information, children gravitate towards the person who they think needs the most support. In many cases, that person is their mother. Typically men are socialized not to react emotionally; therefore, children are led to believe they are not affected. Accordingly, children seek to console the most distraught, most emotional person and in many cases, that is the mother. When they seek to do so, by default, they pick a side. However, if the children pick a side that is one thing. But, when they are forced to pick a side that is a totally different issue!

Picking Sides

Too often children are forced to "pick a side," which is down-right wrong. Adults should never place their children in a "me or them" scenario. Attempts to punish an ex by disrupting their relationship with their children and undermining their authority as a parent are quite common.

When this occurs, some adults go a step further and provide detailed negative information to the children, hoping the children will see the other parent as the "bad guy." One parent will often attempt to utilize the children to adjudicate the separation and divorce. These different attempts are an effort to force the children to pick a side.

Parents who seek to use the children as pawns in the divorce game, also seek validation from the children. The parent wants the children to know the other parent was wrong, did wrong, acted wrong, etc. The parent wants the children to identify which parent is the victim and which parent is the offender. The parent wants the children to validate their position.

Never should a Dad position himself in such a way that he looks for validation by his children. If the Dad is the one who violated the marriage vows or if the Dad is the one that committed whatever transgression, then, as mentioned earlier, he must take responsibility for his actions. That does not mean he has to provide the lurid details to his children, but, he must take responsibility for his actions and seek to make the necessary amends to atone for his behavior.

The thing the Dad should not do is seek to justify his actions or behavior. If the Dad is the offender, no amount of blame shifting or projection is going to compensate for his indiscretion. That is not the time to tell his children how unhappy he was in the marriage. That is not the time to tell his children of how bad a wife their mother was. That is not the time to tell his children anything negative about their mother as an excuse or justification for his behavior. The Dad's manner of addressing his transgression with his children, which led to the obliteration of his children's security blanket, will inform their self-worth, self-identification and self-esteem.

The children will blame themselves and wonder how the Dad could have committed what he did to "them." Children often personalize the undisciplined actions of their Dad and internalize them. While I have focused on the errant behavior of the father, clearly, men are not the only one who violates marriage vows. However, for the purpose of this book, that is my focus. I am currently focused on the intersection between a Dad and a Divorce and in this case, his decision to violate his vows and decimate his marriage.

The bottom line is if you are man enough to make a decision, be man enough to stand alone and face into its headwinds. One of the things I have always said to my son is no matter what I did; I always faced the results of my decisions and took responsibility for them. I did so because no matter what, I should have a valid reason for doing it or else, I should not have done it. Why do I bring that up? If you make a decision to violate, not live up to or ignore your vows and you do so, then be man enough to "face the music," knowing you had a reason which made sense in one of your heads at the time. It is not necessary for others to agree with your reasons, nor do you have to divulge your reasons.

As a man, never do anything unless you have a reason, preferably a well thought out reason that includes how you will manage the situation if it does not turn out positively. You are a grown man. You are big enough to make a decision. You are man enough to do what you want to do, in spite of anyone else. So, stay with that and be man enough to stand up and face into the headwinds.

However, I know a lot of men reading this are saying to themselves that the mother is generally the one who tries to make children pick a side. You are thinking she recruits her children to her side so they see the Dad as a "terrible" human being. She wants them to see her as the victim. You opine this is often necessary as the mother seeks custody of the children.

The more she can make the children see her as the victim and feel sorry for her, the more likely they will "choose" her over the father.

While I will not disagree that some women are guilty of forcing their children to pick a side, I will also say it is not exclusive to women. However, and more importantly, I will say to you, be a man. Man up. You are not responsible for what she does. You control you. You cannot worry about what she is doing or going to do. You do the right thing. When it is all said and done, you will be judged for the works done in your body, not for what someone else did.

> *God will repay each one according to his deeds* (Romans 2:6).

So, do not worry about what she does. As I said earlier in the book, I firmly believe if you are doing the right thing by your ex and your children and if you are doing those things which bring peace, then if she does go to war initially, she will soon call it off and see the value of working with you and not against you.

After my divorce, my ex poured her heart out to my children. She cried in front of them. She grieved in front of them. This behavior encouraged my children to see me as a bully and to hate me for destroying the marriage.

I did not return fire with fire. I did not call them to my house and try to defend myself. I focused on my actions. I did not worry about what she did. I held up a standard for myself.

Whatever I did and whatever she did that caused the demise of our marriage, was not for our children to worry about. What our children needed to know was neither of us was going anywhere, they were not the cause of the marriage dissolution and they were loved. Period.

So, I waited. I gave it time. I allowed my children to hate me. I allowed my children to distance themselves from me. I allowed my children to blame me. I waited. Was it easy? No. But, I had a plan. I needed the rawness to play itself out. I needed time to take the edge off the emotion. After a while, I reached out to my children and sat down to speak with them.

Here is what I said to them:

"I am not going to get into the details of why your mother and I are no longer married. While it is easy to say it was my fault or it was her fault, the truth is it was both of our fault. The details are none of your business. That is between me and your mother. The thing you two need to know is I love you with my whole heart, as does your mother. You also need to know I am not going anywhere. I am not moving. I am staying local and you are welcome at my house whenever you like. As a matter of a fact, it is not my house, it is our house. Therefore, I would like you to pick out the colors for the bathroom. I would like you to come with me to pick out furniture for the house. I would like you to come with me when I go grocery shopping so I always have everything you like to eat. Finally, you need to know while your mother and I could not make our marriage work, we are both committed to co-parenting and staying friends. You have my word the two of you will always motivate me to work my hardest to be the best Dad I can be, whether or not I was the best husband."

I was not going to make my children choose between me and their mother. I was not waiting in the wings to tell my story and make their mother look bad. I understood my children needed both of us in their lives. Though I no longer chose to spend the rest of my life with their mother, she would always be their mother and I was not going to ask them to make a choice.

The concept of asking a child to choose between a mother and a father is like asking your child to choose between one their legs or arms. Just like in our physical body, both the arm and leg have a vital use and responsibility for the proper functioning of one's body, both children's parents have a vital use and responsibility in the proper functioning and development of a child. So, here is where the Dad's relationship with the children is most important. It is your job to co-parent and work on the relationship. It is your job to be present. It is your job to refuse to be drummed out of their life. Hang on as if your life depends on it—because it does.

Your children are your life and your life's work. Your children are the one thing that can never be taken from you and never denied to you. While you may not always earn your children's affection, respect or admiration, they will always remain your responsibility and your children. Try as they might, no one can take away the fact that you fathered them and are tasked, by God, to be accountable for them. Your children are your present and your future. Your children are your legacy and the way your life continues even after you pass.

> *Behold, children are a heritage from the Lord, the fruit of the womb is a reward. Like arrows in the hand of a warrior, so are the children of one's youth. Happy is the man who has his quiver full of them* (Psalm 127:3–5).

Life is not just working every day or accumulating "things." Life is giving life beyond your own. Your children are too important for you not to be engaged in their lives. Your children are so important that you must fight for them! You must fight to protect them. You must fight to provide for them. You must fight to be a priest for them. If not you, who? You have a responsibility to fight for your children and to protect your children. This responsibility is not dependent on their mother's actions. This responsibility is not dependent on their actions. In fact, it is often in spite of their actions.

Model Dad

In 2 Samuel 13, the Bible recounts the story of David and his son Absalom. In this passage, Absalom, avenged his sister of a heinous action towards her, by one of their own brothers. This infighting among his children caused David tremendous pain. Ultimately, Absalom murdered his brother, then fled and took refuge with one of his father's enemies. Yet, David wept for his son.

> *...and the soul of King David longed to go forth unto Absalom* (2 Samuel 13:39).

As the story unfolds, Absalom positioned himself against his father and plotted to overthrow his father, the king. When Absalom attacked, David fled from his son. He did not flee from his son because he was afraid of him. He fled so his son may live. David refused to allow his son, in his youthful ignorance, to jeopardize his own future by putting David in a position to do him harm. So, rather than get into a fight with him, David, the king, chose to retreat. He chose to walk away from all his "things," so that his son may live.

In 2 Samuel 16:22, Absalom went so far as to publicly have sex with one of David's wives. Absalom plotted to overthrow David. David's military advisors counseled David to rein him in. They counseled David to strike, in an effort to retain his kingdom. David was willing to lose his kingdom, for the sake of his son. When Absalom finally brought the war to David, David instructed his men, in 2 Samuel 18:5, to "deal gently for my sake with the young man..." Through all his son's anger, rebellion and "acting up," David allowed his love, and not his emotion, to rule his actions.

David did not allow bad counsel or youthful ignorance to remove him from his son's life. David did not allow the actions of his son to dictate the actions of a Dad. David got it. David understood his role as provider, protector and priest toward his son. Even though his son rejected David's efforts to be a good Dad, David never stopped trying to be a great Dad. David knew his son's very life depended on David remaining focused on his role as a great Dad. David was not concerned about what others thought. David was not concerned about teaching his son a lesson. David was not concerned about winning or losing. David was concerned about showing his son love, no matter what.

At one point David chose to flee, rather than get into a bad situation with a child filled with anger and emotion. David did not have a point to prove. How many times should we have walked away instead of getting into a confrontation with our child? How many times should we have let love, not pride, guide our actions, reactions and interactions?

Ultimately, Absalom was killed. Absalom was killed because of his own actions. Absalom was killed because he could not avoid the Word of God.

Honor thy father and thy mother: that thy days may he long upon the land which the Lord thy God giveth thee (Exodus 20:12).

Absalom's actions brought their own judgment. David did not kill his son. He did not kill him with his mouth, nor did he kill him with his hand. Instead, he loved him despite how Absalom acted. When David was informed of Absalom's death, he uttered one of the most moving and emotion laden expressions in the Bible, found in 2 Samuel 18:33.

O my son Absalom, my son, my son, Absalom! If only had died instead of you, O Absalom, my son, my son (2 Samuel 18:33)!

This is a Dad. This is the emotion of father who has lost a child. This lament shows David's love for his child was greater than all the bad Absalom did and said. However, while love ruled David, David understood anger ruled his son. David did all he could to diffuse the anger. David did all he could to allow the anger to subside. But ultimately, the anger was too great and David was not able to overcome his son's anger with his own love. Sometimes, no matter what you do, you cannot remove your child's anger. Sometimes, you have to give it to God and pray God will deal with your child's anger, while you love them through it.

Expected Anger

Anger can make a child determine you are their enemy. Anger can cloud vision and cause irrational actions. When divorce occurs, many children are angry. Many children are confused. They look for someone to blame and often they blame the biggest person they see. They blame the one they thought was in control.

This is no different than when people blame God for deadly tornados, hurricanes and tsunamis. Because God is so big and in control, they suppose him to be responsible if anything bad that happens. The same applies to the way our children look at us, as Dads. We are so large and in control, clearly we could have stopped it, if we wanted.

After I got divorced, my children were no different. They were angry at me. They demanded to know why I allowed the divorce to happen. They wanted to know why I did not use my powers to stop this terrible thing from happening. My son was angry and lashed out. He acted out, becoming rebellious and defiant. Yes, there were many days I wanted to grab him by the shirt collar, but I knew I had to give him space. Did I handle him the right way all the time? No. I was not perfect in how I managed him. In hindsight, there were a number of things I could have done better. In hindsight, had I understood that love, patience and understanding should guide my interactions, much like David, things could have gone smoother.

There were days I should have retreated. There were days I should have wept and looked the other way, as my son did things to purposely anger or antagonize me. Sometimes, as men, we are too caught up in "being a man" that we forget to "be a Dad." I was guilty of that. I called myself showing my son I was the Alpha Male, when what my son really needed was for me to be the Dad Male. I will always know I could have been more like David towards my son. I could have shown more love to help love him through his anger. I failed with my son, but you do not have to fail with yours. And, if you failed with yours, as I did, then get up off the floor, dust yourself off, learn from your lessons and try, try again. As long as you live and breathe and as long as your son lives and breathes, you have a chance to make it right. If you have more than one child, take each one at a time and save each one. Focus on your son, but not at the expense of your other children. You are talented and can do multiple things at once, so gain inspiration from David and save your son from you and himself.

Daughter's Needs

If you have a daughter, as I do, remember she is now looking to you to help establish what is acceptable and unacceptable in her own life. She will look at many things about how you act and behave to inform her own self-esteem and self-image.

According to Dr. Linda Nielsen, a professor of educational and adolescent psychology at Wake Forest University and the author of Father-Daughter Relationships: Contemporary Research & Issues (2013) and Between Fathers & Daughters: Enriching and Rebuilding Your Adult Relationship (2012), "Fathers have a far-reaching influence on their daughters' lives—both negative and positive. Women miss out if they neglect the bond they have with their fathers. And while fathers may find it easier to relate to and connect with their sons, they should make the effort to build a close relationship with their daughters, too."

Additionally, according to Michael Austin, associate professor of philosophy at Eastern Kentucky University and editor of Fatherhood - Philosophy for Everyone: The Dao of Daddy:

"The type of men that women date and have long-term relationships with is also directly related to the kind of relationship a girl has with her father. Obviously, the hope is that the father figure in a girl's life will aim to skew that young lady's opinions of men in a positive way. 'He must, first and foremost, treat his daughter with respect and love. Whether or not he is married to or still together with his daughter's mom, showing respect to her mother is essential as well,' explains Austin. 'He must also value women as human beings, and not as persons to be used. Daughters will see what their dads believe about women by how they value and respect women, or by how they fail to do so.'"

Your daughter will watch as you communicate with her mother and it will inform her identity as she grows into a woman. Is she already grown or already a late stage teen? Never too late to re-inform who she is based on her father! The very construct of what a woman is, and should be, is informed by her father.

While it is important to be a role model for your son, which is crucial, please recognize your daughter needs your attention too. She is watching you and learning her value based on your actions and words. Your treatment of her mother, and other women, speak volumes about a woman's worth and will inform her perception and self-worth.

You must understand the significant impact your behavior has on your daughter's self-image and how it influences the quality of relationships she chooses. This forms the construct for her perceptions as she journeys into the world of womanhood.

For Christmas one year, my daughter bought me a plaque that read: "Dads—a daughter's first love." I was blown away when she presented it to me. I knew I was fighting for my daughter's image of men and positive view of relationships. I wanted to make sure she did not see me treat her mother with disrespect and correspondingly believe it was the new normal. I wanted to make sure she received love and validation, so she did not seek it in the bed of some young kid who cared more about conquest than love.

As a typical male, I had to get hit in the head with a brick to really get this. I did not really get how impactful I was in my daughter's life until we had a conversation when she turned 17. During the conversation she told me her entire life she put me on a pedestal. She shared how she felt I was invincible and I was her first love. She shared she thought I could do no wrong. But then came the divorce and my subsequent actions. She felt she got lost in the shuffle. She felt I forgot about her and did not love her anymore. I was blown away. As hard as I tried to make sure she knew I loved her, and as hard as I tried to make sure she knew I was there for her, she still felt I no longer loved her. She wondered if I loved a new girlfriend more than her. She wondered if she had done something wrong. She wanted to spend time with me, but I was always working. She wanted to go to Daddy- Daughter Dances, but I was always too busy. She wanted to just hang out with me at my house, but did not happen, either.

Interestingly, I considered myself giving her space. I figured if she wanted to come over my house, she would let me know. I would not force her as she was old enough to make up her own mind. When she would come over, she would stay in her room with the door closed, on her phone or on her computer. I did not pressure her. I tried to give her space. I tried to respect her age and treat her as an adult.

When she wanted to go over her friend's houses, I always said yes. I was accommodating and lenient. In my mind, I was being a good dad by not forcing her to deal with me. I thought she knew I was there for her, if she needed me.

Guess what?

I failed!

I blew it! Why? Because I did all that without asking her if that was the way she wanted to be treated. I failed because it was all about what I thought and what I interpreted as the best way to manage our complex relationship.

What a dope! As smart as I was, yet I missed one major lesson! My daughter wanted me to fight for her and I failed. I did not fight for her attention, for her presence and for her affection. I saw it as me giving space. She perceived that I giving up.

Do not make the same mistake I made. Fight for your daughter. Fight for her attention and her affection. Talk to her. Ask her how she wants you to show your love. When she tells you—do it.

Son's Needs

As it relates to your son, remember, he sees you as a role model. In you, he finds the man he aspires to be or the one he promises he will never be. Which one is it in your case?

Your son, will be a younger version of you. Even if he does not wish to be, he cannot help it. Are you abusive to his mother? He will likely be abusive in his relationships. After all, we are the "how to" book our children read day in and day out.

Before our children learn to read words, they learn to read actions. This first lesson to an impressionable mind is a lasting one. Perhaps the most lasting one. Armed with this reading skill, our children read everything. They read our facial expressions, our body language, our moods, our gestures. Our children learn what to love, what to hate, what to fear, and what to embrace by watching us. As much time as they spend on their phones, they spend ten times that amount, if not a hundred, reading us. Children see everything. We may not notice, but children are always watching. They may have their heads down as they text, play games or watch videos, but they are watching and reading. They are reading our voices and our silence.

As we move down the road of divorce, our children, due to the stressful environment, find their reading skills enhanced and highly sensitized. They are thrust into constant read and interpret mode. They read everything about the situation and unfortunately, often make erroneous interpretations. They color their interpretations with input from others and these interpretations inform their behavior and attitudes.

Your son will use his interpretations to define himself. He sees you as the definition of a man. You have undoubtedly told him you are a man and admonished him to be man. He now begins to utilize the measuring stick you carved for him. As he reads you, he will react to his interpretation by eschewing his interpretation of your actions or embracing his interpretations of your actions.

If you are captivated by your job, with never enough time to spend with the family? He will likely be the same way. I love the way the song "Cats in the Cradle" by Harry Chapin, sums it up. If you do not know the song, I encourage you to "Google" its lyrics.

During your journey down the divorce path, just remember, what your son sees, he becomes. Take the time to work on your relationship. Take the time to do the right thing, for the sake of your children. Your children are watching, they are reading, they are taking mental notes and they are measuring their own self-worth by your actions.

Your children are depending on you to set the boundaries of their lives.

> *Children, obey your parents in the Lord, for this is*
> *right. Honor your father and mother—which is the*

first commandment with a promise that it may go well with you and that you may enjoy long life on the earth (Ephesians 6:1–3).

These words, which Iam commanding you today, shall he on your heart. You should teach them diligently to your children and talk of them when you sit in your house and when you walk by the way and when you lie down and when you rise up (Deuteronomy 6:6–7).

Your instructions are clear and your children are counting on you to fulfill them. They do not even know why. They just know they look to you to teach them, to instruct them, to protect them, to provide for them. They are born with this innate expectation.

Hence, your relationship with your children is even more critical as a result of the divorce. Work on it. Pay attention to it. Do not allow an unfortunate and unnecessary war to distract you from the most important thing, the health and well-being of your children.

I allowed myself to be distracted from my relationship with my son. I was distracted by what I wanted him to become. I was distracted by my plans for him. I was distracted by what I imagined my son would do better than I. I unfairly placed expectations on him, based on my own desires. I needed him to be something and someone, in order to validate me.

I had good intentions, but, honestly, my intentions really do not matter. Many parents, Dads in particular, ruin their children's lives with good intentions. Differently than with my daughter, I did not give my son space, I crowded him. I needed him to be strong, resilient, resourceful and courageous. I needed him to make better decisions. I needed him to have a better education. I even obsessed about the perception of friends, coworkers and family if he did not achieve these things. Conversely, I inwardly smiled about how he (translated me), would be received if he just did these basic things "I" wanted for him.

KEN GORDON

On Father's Day one year, my son wrote me a letter saying he did not want to be anything like me. He said what he wanted was to be "him." Because the person I was, was too stressful and too much of a leap from where he saw himself. Therefore, he decided he wanted to go in the opposite direction.

I was furious. How dare he!? What was wrong with me? I was a good dad. While I did not succeed at my marriage to his mother, at least I had not abandoned him and his sister after the marriage was over. Who did he think he was? (brick to head) He was my son, not my clone.

I treated him like he was supposed to be me. I treated him like everything about him did not matter. I treated him like whatever he became, whether it was ideal to me or not, was not be good enough. I fancied myself as a good dad, but it was more like I was just a decent provider, who happened to be his father. Big difference. A father is that biological entity that has the ability to contribute to bringing life into the world. A dad is one who appreciates the life brought into the world for exactly what it is, without judgment.

My son purposely did everything he could to underscore he was not me. He purposely engaged in activities, behaviors and lifestyles he knew were opposite of me. Was I angry? Yes. Did I understand? Not at that time. But, my righteous anger and inability to understand did not stop or dissuade his efforts. He was on a mission. He was going to show me he was stronger and more committed to being him, than I was to making him me.

As a divorced man, I was already at a disadvantage, due to the separated households. In front of me he would behave in a manner that minimized confrontation between the two of us. Whether he liked it or not, he understood who was the Alpha Male. He was not ready to physically take me on. However, around his mother and friends, he became the antithesis of my vision of him.

I kept waiting for him "snap out of it." I kept waiting for him to mature. I kept waiting for him see where his choices were leading him. Ultimately, he was not hurting me, but himself, [sound of brakes screeching]

98

Wait a second—I thought the Bible instructed me to be the protector? It does. It even provides for protecting our children from themselves. Our role is clear and it is beyond contestation. Our responsibility is to protect our children. While it may be easier to protect them from a snarling animal or a vicious street gang than from themselves, it is no less important.

As David did with Absalom, it was my responsibility to love him, no matter what he did. When he tries to go to war with me, it is my responsibility to retreat, so we both may live. When he takes something, which is precious to me and defiles it, it is my responsibility to look beyond the act and understand the angst. When he seeks vengeance, it is my responsibility to seek peace.

There is no doubt having children is challenging and rewarding. Our responsibility is to always understand we must love our children and their future more than we love ourselves. True, unconditional love, which is what we should possess for our children, is all about sacrifice and the willingness to love, no matter what.

As a divorced Dad, there is much understanding, patience and love required to understand how your actions, in concert with those of your former spouse, affect your children. You must show love and compassion towards your children. You must commit to do whatever is necessary to establish and enhance your relationship with your children. If it means some days you must retreat, then retreat. If it means some days you must shut up, then shut up. If it means some days you must swallow your pride, then swallow. If it means you must change your vision, future and plans, then change.

As a divorced Dad, there is truly nothing more important in your life than your relationship with your children. Make the right decision when it comes to cultivating your relationship as a father. Ultimately, it is the most important investment you can make into all of your family.

CHAPTER 8

HIDE AND SEEK

Take precaution when dating. This book is about your relationship with your children, so let me broach a very important topic regarding your children: Post-divorce dating.

> *If they cannot exercise self-control, they should marry. For it is better to marry than to burn with passion* (1 Corinthians 7:9).

> *He who finds a wife finds a good thing, and obtains favor from the Lord* (Proverbs 18:22).

The process of "seeking" is better known as dating. However, for a Christian, dating is not as carefree and cavalier as it is for those not professing salvation. One professing salvation has several things they must consider, if they choose to "seek" companionship.

First, you must understand the Word of God's stance on marrying someone who does not profess salvation.

> *Do not be unequally yoked with unbelievers* (2 Corinthians 6:14–15).

Second, you must understand the Word of God's stance on the priority of the relationship, as it relates to Christ. God must be first, above all else.

Jesus declared, "Love the Lord your God with all your heart and with all your soul and with all your mind." This is the first and greatest commandment... (Matthew 22:37).

God must come before the dating relationship, your job and your children. God must be first, for only when God is first, can the rest of your life fall into place.

But seek first the kingdom of God and His righteousness, and all these things will he added unto you (Matthew 6:33).

Third, you must understand the Word of God's stance on choosing the right person.

Trust in the Lord with all your heart and do not lean on your own understanding in all your ways acknowledge Him and He will direct your paths (Proverbs 3:5–6).

When you are dating, consult God about the person. Avoid using "I-sight" when making a decision about your relationship. Rather, remember your 20/20 Character Vision and trust your Father, who is in Heaven, to lead you to the right person and to bless your relationship.

As you embark upon the relationship, remember not to defile the relationship by introducing sex before the Word of God instructs. Also, remember to be a Spiritual leader and priest. Lead by example. Pray together. Worship together. Study together.

But, I am getting ahead of myself. You are divorced. You have children. You have appropriately consulted God and believe he has released you to date. Now what? What are the first things to be considered? More importantly, your loins aside, what are the most important things to be considered as a divorced dad?

The question is not will you start dating, rather, when will you start dating. Unless your divorce left you so emotionally scarred, psychologically exhausted and totally misanthropic, you will certainly date one day. Do not rush this day, but know it will come.

I knew I would one day date again, although, I was confident I would never remarry. However, I was willing to wait to put myself back out there again. I was afraid, lacked confidence and was not looking forward to the "games" that often come with dating. But, I knew I would eventually garner the courage to wade back into the dating pool.

> I have the right to do anything, "you say—but not everything is beneficial." I have the right to do anything—but not everything is constructive (1 Corinthians 10:23).

In addition to your ability to do it, there is also the issue of the proper dispensation, the proper time according to all things in your life, to include your children.

> There is a time for everything, and a season for every activity under the heavens: a time to be born and a time to die, a time to plant and a time to uproot, a time to kill and a time to heal, a time to tear down and a time to build, a time to weep and a time to laugh, a time to mourn and a time to dance, a time to scatter stones and a time to gather them, a time to embrace and a time to refrain from embracing, a time to search and a time to give up, a time to keep and a time to throw away, a time to tear and a time to mend, a time to be silent and a time to speak, a time to love and a time to hate, a time for war and a time for peace (Ecclesiastes 3:1–8).

You must also seek to do those things that make for peace.

So then, we must pursue what promotes peace and
what builds up one another (Romans 14:19).

Though you—in all your adult splendor—may want to do something, you must consider the impact on the other parts of your life. You do not live in a bubble, nor is it all about you.

When you are tempted to make things post-divorce all about you, please remember these three letters: D A D. It was enough that you focused on your sanity, happiness and future when you decided to go through with the divorce. I get it. I am not apologizing for doing it and am not asking you to apologize either.

However, understand that your pursuit of happiness caused disruption to your children's identity, self-image and world, as they knew it. Given this occurrence, I would ask you to consider how you can mitigate further disruption to their lives.

Am I asking you to put your life on hold? Am I asking you to ignore your own needs? Am I asking you to suppress your desires? To a degree, I absolutely am. To a degree I am telling you when you have children, you make the decision it is not all about you. When you have people for whom you are responsible and of whom you are chosen to be their protector, provider and priest, then, yes, there are sacrifices you must make, even post-divorce. And this extends to dating.

You will be ready to date before your children are ready for you to date. They require much more healing time. They require much more processing time. Remember, they are not as mature as you and are not as emotionally developed. So, it takes their not-fully developed minds longer to digest certain things. And when that certain thing is a new woman occupying the space once reserved for their mother, then add time on to that.

While your children may smile and be agreeable, my counseling and personal experience suggests they are often internally conflicted.

When I decided I was ready to get back into the world of dating, I approached my children and asked their opinion. They were both gracious and accepting. They both intimated their support and willingness to accept my decision. I walked away from the conversation thinking, "Wow, my children are so mature and understanding. They really are cool."

I mistakenly believed what they said. Big Mistake.

While I have no doubt they believed what they said at the time, it is one thing to say something in the absence of reality and another thing when that reality shows up at the front door. Only when your conversation becomes flesh will you truly know how your children will respond.

In my children I received two different responses. One of my children became passive-aggressive. Passive-aggression is a type of behavior or personality characterized by indirect resistance to the demands of others and an avoidance of direct confrontation, as in procrastinating, pouting, or misplacing important materials. The other child became ambivalent. Much like Buridan's Donkey, this child was unable to make up their mind on whether to be happy for me or mad at me. While both initially professed support, neither were able to bring themselves to fulfill that promise. But I do not fault them. I get it. I totally get it.

The transition is a delicate one, fraught with pitfalls and bear traps. This transition is a potential mine-field chock full of deadly snares, which could cause you and your potential new interest, incalculable stress and anxiety. This situation, though difficult to avoid, can offer unique and special opportunities to demonstrate to your children their perpetual importance to you. Instead of them feeling they have lost their dad, if done effectively, this situation can provide bonding opportunities.

So, how do you manage that? You play Hide and Seek. When I got divorced, I was very careful not to allow my children to meet every woman I dated. One of the worst things is for your children, who are doing all they can to digest the divorce, is to now have to digest some new person on the scene.

It's just too much!

You should not look at it like you are "sneaking," rather like you have to protect your children from information overload. You have to protect them from their own emotions. You also have to protect yourself from their perceptions.

As I have indicated previously, your children's perception of you matters. So much of our behavior informs a child's view of themselves, perception of the world and understanding of boundaries. While the internet, peers, and social media have inserted themselves into our children's cognitive realities, they have not completely eliminated the effects parents have on children's perceptions, lives and identities.

Parents play a huge role in shaping children's perceptions, images, realities and views. In some cases, we see children mimic their parents, in others we see them utilize their parents to forge a new reality and yet in others we see them use their parents to define an opposite view. Regardless of how children respond to parental stimuli, the fact is parents have influence on their children. So, when it comes to dating, as a divorced dad, you must remember the things you do will influence and impact your children.

In her blog, "Dating, Divorce, and Your Kids," Heather Setrakian, M.A., co-investigator in eHarmony Labs' Marriage and Family Development Study and co-creator of the Interpersonal Chemistry and Communication in Dating studies for eHarmony Labs, states:

"Children may have more trouble adjusting to their fathers' dating relationships than their mother's. This may be because of the diverted attention in the wake of limited time together due to custody issues. Another possibility is the potential for the new relationship to be the cause of the parent's divorce."

When I began dating, I was very careful who my children met. It took me quite a while to allow my children to meet anyone I dated. I did not date a lot of people and I was not trying to pollinate all the flowers. I was cognizant that even one person, to my children, was a lot.

I was keenly aware my time with them was already limited, due to the custodial situation, so aside from wanting to date, I also wanted to spend a lot of time with my children. It was not really a conundrum. The choice was easy! Spend all the time with my children that the custody agreement would allow and focus on my love life during the off times. Additionally, to Ms. Setrakian's point, my children were dubious of whether the person to which I introduced them was "the one" that caused the marriage between me and their mother to fail. So, I needed to be sentient, as it related to my children. I needed to be careful who I allowed them to meet.

If your children see you go from person to person, as you date and seek to find healing for your own hurt and pain, then they could easily lose respect for you. Their perception may be that you are acting improper. During counseling sessions, I have actually heard children say their father was acting like a slut. Nothing is worse than when your own children form a negative opinion of you, based on your actions. It's one thing for them to form a negative opinion of you based on misinformation. It's a whole different ball game when they receive their perception after watching you!

After my divorce, I would not allow my children to know who I was dating. I made very sure they did not cross paths at my house. I made sure we did not cross paths in public. I was careful. Was it sometimes frustrating to the woman I was dating? Yeah, I am sure it was. And for the one that became frustrated, she also found that her nights cleared up pretty fast, because once I saw that my attempts to protect my children and make sure I went the extra mile to shield them, were frustrating to her, she was in the wind. See ya. You are clearly not the one.

When my children visited with me, I was careful not to have late night visitors. Trust me, if you think your children do not hear the door opening at two in the morning, you are sadly mistaken and you are underestimating them.

Managing the divorce journey of your children plays hides and seeks with your personal, romantic life. Shield them. Protect them. Do not give them too much information to process. Do not let them see too much. What they see, they cannot unsee. What they hear, they cannot unhear. So, put your romantic needs behind your children's mental and psychological needs. Guard your children's perception of you and protect the sacredness of your standing in their eyes. While you may think their mother has effectively reduced your standing in their eyes, there is something about children that makes them want to love their parent… no matter what. It's called unconditional love.

Love is a special and complicated emotion that is often difficult to understand and articulate. Many people believe love is about the heart, but it is actually about the brain. There are different forms and styles of expressing love. The Ancient Greeks came up with four terms (agape, phileo, storge, and eros) to symbolize the four types of love.

The first is agape love. This is an unconditional love that sees beyond the outer surface and accepts the recipient for whom they are, regardless of their flaws, shortcomings or faults. It's the type of love Christ has for us and the kind he instructs us to have for others. This kind of love is all about sacrifice as well as giving and expecting nothing in return. It is a committed and chosen love.

The second is phileo love. Phileo love refers to an affectionate, warm and tender platonic love. It makes you desire friendship with someone.

The third love is storge love. It is a kind of family and friendship love. This is the love that parents naturally feel for their children or the love that members of the family have for each other. Storge love is unconditional, accepts flaws or faults and ultimately drives you to forgive. It is committed, sacrificial and makes you feel secure, comfortable and safe.

The fourth love is eros. Eros is a passionate and intense love that arouses romantic feelings; it is the kind that often triggers "high" feelings in a new relationship and makes you say, "I love him/her." It focuses more on self instead of the other person.

As it relates to your children, their "storge" love is subject to repression as a result of fear, anger, anxiety and disappointment. However, it is generally repressed, not removed. Let their mother say whatever she wants to say. If you have worked on your relationship with your children and continue to do so when possible, they will know. And guess what? When the time is right, they will return to you.

Give them space. Let them be angry. Let them step away. Just know, if you have brought them up right, they will be back. Just do not do anything to chase them away or keep them away longer than necessary. Play hide and seek with your personal life when traversing the divorce path.

Hide your relationships from your children until the time is right and seek to know the appropriate and best time to reveal someone about which you are serious. You are not hiding because you are being sneaky or in an effort to deceive. Rather, you are hiding to protect and shield your children. Remember, your children are still adjusting to you being single and likely still hoping you and their mother will get back together. Introducing a significant other too soon can have damaging psychological and emotional effects.

According to Tina B. Tessina, Ph.D. (aka "Dr. Romance"), licensed psychotherapist and author of "The Unofficial Guide to Dating Again," children should not have any clue that their parents are dating. With thirty years of counseling experience, Dr. Tessina says, "Until the relationship is a serious one, children shouldn't know about dad's new partner."

Nancy Fagan, divorce consultant and owner of San Diego's Divorce Help Clinic, says that six months is essential, but it must be six months of exclusive dating. For some families the time may be longer. "If any of the children are still in pain over the separation or divorce, dads will need to wait longer," Fagan says. "This is to eliminate confusion while children process their pain and grieve the loss of their former family unit."

Hide the relationship. Ensure it is serious. Seek the right time to introduce the new person. Wait for your children to heal, grieve and begin to mentally move forward.

Do not rush it.

When I was ready to date, I sought God for direction.

In all thy ways acknowledge him, and he shall direct thy paths (Proverbs 3:6).

This area—especially this area—absolutely the application of Scripture.

I personally waited until I felt my children had healed and could mentally handle seeing me with another woman. Even then, I was initially self-conscious and nervous about how they would react and respond. I kept checking with them to make sure they were okay.

I did not flaunt the other person, nor did I show excessive PDA (Public Displays of Affection) around them.

Was this right? Should I have just thrown them into the ice-cold pool and let them adjust? Perhaps, but these were "my children" and I cared about their psychological wellbeing. If I was going to err, it was going to be on the side of looking out for them. I was going to err on the side of protecting them.

I dated several women. If one of the relationships did not work out, for whatever reason, I could move on and find another woman to date. If one of the relationships went sour, I could find someone else upon which to lavish my romantic affection. However, if something happened to my children, I could not just move on to new children. If my relationship with my children moved to a point of disrepair, I could not just drop them and find new children on eHarmony.

I was more concerned about my children than whether the person I was dating understood my actions. Do not get me wrong. I was not insensitive to the person I was dating. However, I was upfront in ensuring they knew how important my children, and the relationship with my children, were to me. And you know what? The majority of them respected and admired that.

Beware of the woman who knows you have children but insists upon you putting her before them or who ignores them. The woman you are dating should want to meet your children, but should respect you taking your time and being careful in the introduction. Further, if she has children, she should be equally as careful with you.

You should hide all relationships from your children until you find the person who you believe will be around for the long term. Your children have already lost enough. You should protect them from putting someone in their life they may lose soon thereafter, as well. Hide all relationships from your children to protect their perception and opinion of you. Sometimes children see too much, too soon. Seek God to know the right time and the right person for you and your children's lives.

CHAPTER 9

SAVING OUR SEED

For the children. I want to use this chapter as an opportunity to talk directly to the children of divorce.

To Children of Divorce

Hello! My name is Ken Gordon. I wrote this book for Dads impacted by divorce. I personally went through a divorce and learned a lot about being a better dad. If you would give me a few minutes of your time, I want to share some of the things I learned.

While I am sure you would prefer me to text this to you, there's too much for me to share to read through text. I also do not have your SnapChat, Twitter or Facebook, so I can't share my thoughts with you the way you prefer to be talked to. I also have no clue how to use Instagram or Tumblr, if those are even popular anymore. My daughter promised to show me how to use all the different sites, but we have been pretty busy writing this book, so it has not happened.

I have two children: a son and a daughter. My son is a pretty amazing guy. He loves to write music and loves to rap. My son is the best dancer I have ever seen. I believe he could give the very best dancers out there a run for their money. I do not want to mention who is a good dancer for fear you may not like the person. I will just say he is an excellent dancer. A lot of times before going to a big meeting with my company, I ask him to show me how to do certain dances. He taught me to do the Cupid Shuffle, the Whip, the Nay Nay and the Stanky Leg. He is a good cook and an even better eater! He decided college was not for him, so he went to Job Corps to learn cooking and now is working a good job as a cook. My son is one hundred times better looking than I ever was and a heck of a lot smarter than I am.

My son was fifteen years old when his mother and I divorced. When I got divorced, my son took it pretty hard. He took his mother's side and I am glad he did. He became very protective of her, as he should have. I was always so proud of how he sided with his mom and did everything he could to protect her. My son has never disrespected me, talked back to me or tried to beat me up. But he made it clear he would protect his mother. He did exactly as I taught him.

Boys should ALWAYS protect and look after their mother. Period.

My daughter is also an amazing person. Responsible and mature beyond her years, she is a beautiful person, inside and out. One day I hope she becomes an attorney or some other professional where she can use her analytical and reasoning skills to help her achieve success. She is also an amazingly creative thinker! Recently, she said, "Dad, do you think when dogs see police canine dogs, they run the other way, yelling, 'Uh oh, here comes the Po Po?'"

Yes, you're right; she has an incredible sense of humor.

One of her passions is doing makeup. She does regular makeup for prom or going out or just going to school. But she also does Special EFX makeup. She does makeup that looks like someone beat her up, or slit her throat or shot her in the head. She has already done the Special EFX makeup for a rap music video.

My daughter was twelve when her mother and I divorced.

The divorce devastated her.

Why am I telling you about my children? Because as a Dad, we see our children, and are proud of our children and notice our children more than you realize. Men do not do a good job of showing emotion or affection. We do not do a good job of talking and telling our children how proud we are of them and how much we love them.

I do not know your father and I do not know the circumstances of your parent's divorce. But with all my heart I can tell you, regardless of what happened with your parents, it was not your fault. No matter what you think or even what they may have said. Regardless of if you are imperfect or having problems in school. It doesn't matter what you did in the past or did not do. There is nothing you could have done to stop the divorce. Nothing. Unfortunately, all relationships do not work out, even when the relationship is a marriage.

Just like I know my children and remember so much about them and our lives together, your dad feels the same way. He may not tell you, but I am telling you for him. He may not be good at talking. He may not be good at expressing himself. But, if you could get into his head, you would see him smile every time he thinks of you.

I wrote this book to remind fathers that having a relationship with their children is the most important thing in the world, as a father. I wanted to share with dads all the mistakes I made so they would not make the same mistakes or if they have already made them, to go back and correct them.

In the process of talking to dads about being better fathers during or after a divorce, I wanted to take a moment and talk to the children. So many times we talk to the parents and counsel them and forget about the children. We forget your feelings and thoughts. That is one of the reasons I asked my daughter to write a chapter in the book, so dads could hear from children and understand how divorce impacts them. I hope your dad reads my daughter's chapter and takes it to heart.

We can be honest with one another, correct? Okay, here goes: I believe you are hurting.

You are likely blaming yourself for your parent's breakup and divorce, even if you have not been able to actually put your finger on how you could be responsible. You are probably thinking a lot about what you may have done:

Maybe if you would have been a better child. Maybe if you would have cleaned your room. Maybe if you would not have gotten in trouble at school. There are a lot of maybes. But the truth is, none of those maybes matter. None of them are true. You could have been the perfect child and your parents would have still divorced.

Maybe you are going through it now. Maybe it's all going on around you and you are trying to make sense of it. Maybe there is yelling and arguing or maybe there is just silence. Either way, the same thing applies. If it got to this point, it had nothing to do with you.

I am sure you are wondering and maybe even praying: "God please do not let my parents get a divorce. Please talk some sense into them. I know they love each other. God, if you do this, then I will not talk back or I will clean my room or I will not get in trouble in school."

I get it. If the divorce is not final, there is hope. However, let me tell you three things: 1) regardless of whether it happens or not, just know it is not your fault, 2) please know that no matter what happens next, your parents love you, and 3) no matter what has happened to you and no matter what your parents have done or said, God loves you. He sees you. He has a plan for your life and He loves you. It may not seem like it right now. But if you give Him a chance to show you, you will see He is, and has always been there for you.

Wherever you are and whatever your situation, I am praying for you. You are important to God and when you get through this, you will be so much stronger and better. Yes, it hurts and will hurt. Yes it sucks. Why can't two people that love each other work it out? Only God knows. But, please know whether your parents are going through divorce or already divorced, you will stop hurting and you will get through it. Just do not blame yourself. It is not your fault.

You could have done everything right and even personally escorted your parents to all their meetings and events. You could have moved heaven and earth. You could have been the best kid in the world. Yet, in spite of all of that, there is a good chance your parents would be exactly where they are.

They would either be going through the divorce or already divorced.

What you have got to know is two things: first, what is going on has nothing to do with how much your parents love you. Please,

please know it is about how relationships go and the things that happen in them. It is not just your parents. A lot of people who started off together, then had children, found their relationship in trouble later on. It is not always that someone did something wrong. There are so many different reasons why relationships fail. Right now, it does not make sense to you. Maybe it never will. Maybe you will never know what happened and the truth is, you really should not know.

As a dad who is divorced with children that were hurt, I can tell you most parents really do not want their children to have to deal with everything that comes with getting a divorce. If your parents could work it out, they would and they will. If they cannot, give them grace and know if they could have figured it out or worked it out, they would have.

Second, the divorce has nothing to do with you. It is not, and was not, your fault or the fault of any of your brothers and sisters, if you have them. Maybe you do not feel like you had anything to do with it. If you do not, great.

In the beginning my children thought they could have done something to have prevented their mother and me from getting a divorce. They thought they had something to do with it. However, they very quickly figured out that did not have anything to do with what was happening.

Yes, they still hurt. But at least they did not blame themselves. That was progress and that was important. If I can get you to understand you did not cause the divorce or the problems in your parent's marriage and there was nothing you can do or could have done to make it stop or go away, then you will be doing really good.

Divorce is a confusing thing. How can two people who loved each other so much at one time, now tear your family apart and cause such unhappiness and destruction? How could they be so selfish? How could they be so inconsiderate? You have so many questions. Many of your questions will never be answered, or if they are, not to your satisfaction. So, what do you do?

First, you stop blaming yourself. Yeah, I know, easier said than done. But the truth is that with divorce come a lot of things you may not wish to do. Your parent's divorce was a sign there were problems and issues much bigger and more serious than whether you were a "good" child, kept a clean room or got good grades. Divorce is about two people that no longer wish to live together as husband and wife. It is about two people who believe their only path to true happiness is going separate ways. Unfortunately, the children are often caught in the middle and too often pulled back and forth. Which leads me to the second thing you can do?

Do not take either of your parent's side. Maybe you were in a home where there was abuse, or drug use or things going on where you were being hurt. Maybe one or both of your parents were mean and cruel to you. These are realities. I know not all children were in a household where everything was great. But, even in those situations, do not take a side.

The reason why you should not take one of your parent's side is because while you may be angry and hurting right now, later in your life, the anger will lessen and you will want to forgive the parent whose side you did not take. You will want to forgive them for mistreating you and for mistreating the other parent. Because children were made by God to love their parents unconditionally, when you are angry or filled with hate towards a parent, it eats away at you like no other kind of emotion. When you get older and get a family, it will continue eating away at you.

If one of your parents are mean, cruel, abusive, unfaithful, addicted to drugs or alcohol, or mistreated you sexually, then you cannot spend the mental energy taking a side with the other parent against them. If you want to take a side, take the side of right. Take the side of good.

It is not right for a parent to mistreat their child. It is not natural for a parent to be abusive, cruel, or mean Spirited. So instead of taking the side of the other parent, take the side of good. I promise you your healing will be much easier by taking the side of good versus taking the side of either of your parents.

Another reason you do not want to take the side of one of your parents is if you do, the parent whose side you took will put you in the middle of the relationship or will use you as their therapist. You do not want to be in either position. Both positions are unfair, stressful and put more pressure on you than you are already enduring.

As much as it seems you know who is the cause for a divorce, the truth is, you do not. What you may know or have seen is someone's reaction, but you never saw what initiated it. Like in class when someone does something to another student and the other student reacts and that reaction gets the teacher's attention. The one who reacted gets in trouble while the one who started it sits back smiling. Well, it's kind of like that. Sometimes, when a person is unhappy they will "react." The bigger question is why were they unhappy? That is information you may never have. All you can do is look at one person's reaction and judge. Do not fall for that trap. In a marriage, if something goes wrong, there are two people to blame. No one is blame free. So, do not fall for one of your parent's blaming the other and trying to get you to side with them. They are both your parents and they both love you, in spite of what you may think or the

Next, give grace. What does it mean to give grace? The meaning of the word grace is an act or instance of kindness, courtesy, mercy or leniency. So, to give grace to your parents or dad means to show some mercy and kindness, even though they may not deserve it. The whole act of grace really applies when you do not think someone deserves it. Showing kindness or mercy to someone who deserves it, is not hard. But God wants us to show mercy and kindness to people we do not think deserve it. When we do this, God shows us kindness and mercy when we do not deserve it.

So why is it so important to show grace?

> *Blessed are the merciful far they shall receive mercy*
> (Matthew 5:7).

So, first, it is important to show mercy and grace because the day will come when you need mercy and grace. As it says in Luke 6:31, which we refer to as the "Golden Rule," "Do to others as you would have them do to you."

As much as you may hurt right now, you know one day you will make a big mistake. It may be in the next week, month or year. But one day you will make a mistake or you will do something that causes others pain. When that day comes, you want to be in the position to have someone show you mercy.

If you have been someone who was willing to show mercy to others, they will have no problem showing mercy to you. It is like what goes around comes around or like you will reap what you sow. If that phrase is not familiar to you, please Google it or read Galatians 6:7, which says, "…. a man reaps what he sows." In other words, the things you do to others will eventually come back around to you.

The second reason it is important to give grace and mercy is because your parents are already hurting and feeling guilty. While it may not seem like it on the outside, going through separation or divorce is a horrible experience for parents. They feel hurt, guilty, disappointed and angry. While you may only think of yourself, your parents must think of themselves and how they will move forward and they must think of their children and how they will move forward also.

So, just as you need mercy from time to time, your parents really need it now. They know they have let you down and hurt you. They know they have hurt the family. They already know these things. You being hard on them is not going to make them know it more. It makes them guiltier and hurts all of you even more. As much as you may be angry, disappointed or hurt, your healing will come quicker if you grant grace and mercy to your parents.

The Bible talks about the gospel of grace (Acts 20:24), the importance of grace (Ephesians 2:8–9), the need for grace (Romans 3:23), to whom God gives grace (1 Peter 5:5) and the beauty of grace (Ephesians 1:5–6). Additionally, my reason for asking you to grant grace is not only the Bible, but personal experience.

I needed my children to grant me grace.

When I got divorced, I was very concerned with how my children would handle all the emotions and information being thrown at them. I was concerned how they would treat and view me. I was concerned whether I lost their respect. I felt guilty for disappointing them and making them deal with the situation. Late at night when I was alone, I would ask myself if I was doing the right thing. I would ask myself if I should just stay in the situation, even if I was not happy, for the sake of my children.

However, my children gave me grace. They both told me they knew I was unhappy. They both told me while they wish it did not happen, they understood and forgave me. Their grace and kindness, at a time when they could have been disrespectful and mean, helped me be a better dad. It helped me focus on making sure I treated them and their mother right. The thing about grace is it has a domino effect. When you give grace to your dad, then he can forgive himself and not be caught up in guilt. When he can forgive himself and not be caught up in guilt, it helps him heal and put his focus on treating your mother right, treating you right and making sure he does right.

Grant your parent's grace. They are not perfect and do not always make the right decisions. It is part of being human. It is so much easier right now to be angry and lash out. However, stop thinking about yourself for a moment (as you wish your parents would do) and think of how incredibly difficult this is for them. If one of your parents made a terrible mistake and that mistake brought about the divorce, imagine how guilty and terrible they feel on the inside. If your parents were just not able to make things work, imagine how much of a failure they feel like. No matter what, give grace to your parents. It can make the situation so much easier if you give them grace. That does not mean you are not angry or you are happy with their decisions, it just means you will grant them grace and not punish them more than they are already being punished.

Just as important as grace, is forgiveness. Just like grace, when you give someone forgiveness you do not think deserves it, you are doing what God asks of you. The Lord's Prayer, which is found in Matthew 6, says in verse 12, "forgive our debts, as we forgive our debtors." You cannot be forgiven unless you are one who will and has forgiven. If you want God to forgive you, you must also have a willingness to forgive. Trust me, there will be plenty of times in your life when you will want forgiveness of God, family and friends and you will not deserve it. In this case, just like in the case of grace, grant your parents forgiveness and know they did not intend this to happen. If there were any way they could prevent you from experiencing your pain, they would. By the way, even if none of that was true and you think your parents do not care and would hurt you, then just know that God would not. So, forgive them because God asks us to.

Finally, remember, these two people that ripped the family apart are still your parents and as such, still must be respected and honored. No matter how bad you are hurting, no matter how angry you are, or no matter how much you blame one or the other, they are still your parents.

I've learned a lot and failed many times with my children. This is one of those situations where I failed. Looking back, I now see things I should have done differently. Life is about lessons. You often do not learn your lesson while you are in the midst of your situation. Rather, if you are honest with yourself and seek to be a better person, you can look back on any situation and recognize lessons, which will make you better and help you not repeat the same mistakes.

If I could do it all over again, or if I could advise someone who was going through it right now, I would tell them not to do what I did. While I thought I was allowing it to run its course and waiting for the emotion and anger to die down, it looked like I did not care. It looked like it was not important to me. It looked like I was guilty of everything of which I was being accused. However, none of that was true.

I trusted myself too much. I used my children's love in the wrong way. Instead of fighting for their respect and understanding, I counted on them loving me no matter what, so I waited. I waited and did not think about what they were going through. I waited and did not think about how they were suffering. Sometimes, adults are too smart for our own good. Sometimes adults are so smart until we are just plain dumb.

As a dad, I should have thought more about how my silence was affecting my children. I should have thought more about how effective communication with my children could have saved them a lot of questions and anxiety. I should have been more responsible and more proactive, for the good of my children. I may not have liked what was going on, but instead of ignoring it, I should have addressed it.

No matter what, you should treat your mother way better than your father. After all, she is the one that carried you nine months.

A Message to the Boys

There is something special about the bond between a mother and a son, just like there is something special about the bond between a father and his daughter. Boys are protectors and providers. This is part of who you are. You do not turn on your "male protector instincts" when you turn 21. They are on from the time you are born. You may not know exactly what happened or whose fault it is, however, you should always have your mom's back. Period. You should have your mom's back, as a protector and provider, which is how God made you. If that means you have to protect her from being attacked verbally or physically by your father, then so be it, because your mother is worth it. One thing I know is there is no one who will be there for you like your mother.

I recently read about a guy who went to Utah to hike and mountain bike. He was hiking the canyons and got his arm pinned between an 800-pound boulder and the canyon wall. He was stuck there for five days. He thought he was going to die. He ended up cutting off his arm to escape. After he cut off his arm, he hiked seven miles trying to get back to his car. He was bleeding, cold and exhausted. He was close to death and knew he was going to die. He knew no one would find him because he did not tell anyone he was going to another state to hike and mountain bike. Ultimately, he was rescued. You know how? His mother saved him!

His mother knew he was missing and did whatever was necessary to find her son, because she sensed he was in trouble. That is what mother's do. I encourage you to watch the movie, which is called, "127 Hours." The bottom line is there is something special about a mother and no matter who is at fault or what the children are told, I always believe the mother deserves the respect and grace of her children, especially her sons.

During and after a divorce, some men will threaten and bribe their sons, with money, material goods and promises of support. Some fathers use the fear factor to turn their children against the mother. Some fathers try to force the children to hate the mother or have the same negative feelings as the father. I encourage every child who will read this to reject those terrible and ungodly directions. If your father is so weak and insecure he needs to turn his children against their own mother, he is not a man deserving of your loyalty, belief or support.

It is not your place to judge your mother. It is not your place to position yourself against the person that, through pain and labor, brought you into this world. It is not your place to mistreat the person who would give her life for you and who, for the rest of your life, will be there for you. There is often no right or wrong and no perfect person in any relationship, however, I am convinced if you give your mother grace and respect, and you will always be blessed. Do not allow your father to turn you against your mother or make you mistreat your mother. A mother's heart is much softer than a father's heart and it cannot take rejection by her children, especially her sons.

Anyway, the bottom line with my children is I did not stop reaching out to them. I did not stop being a dad. I did not stop providing for and protecting my children. I did not stop working to stay visible. I refused to go away, no matter how mad they were at me. I bought a new house three blocks away and refused to take a promotion and move. I knew if I could help my children get through this period, they would have a chance to recover and grow from the situation.

So, here you sit. You are somewhere between the throbbing pain of denial and the numbing feeling of acceptance. Find someone with whom you can talk. Preferably a professional, as opposed to a friend at school whose parents also got a divorce. Do what my daughter did and tell your parents you need to talk to someone who can help you navigate the difficulty of the situation. Talk to someone that can help you and not someone that will just nod their head and agree with everything you are saying. During your parents' divorce, it is not good to be alone with your thoughts. Figure out a way to talk to your parents. If you cannot talk to both, talk to whichever one is easier to talk to. But talk to someone!

Millions and millions of children survive divorce and go on to do just fine. While I am sure that does not matter to you because you are not millions and millions of children, I offer that merely because I have hope. I have hope that you and my own children as well, can and will make it through the divorce recovery process without permanent damage.

Just remember your parents are human and make mistakes. If you remember this you will be on your way to feeling better and getting through this tough time in your life.

All of us makes mistakes (James 3:2).

For all have sinned and fall short of the glory of God (Romans 3:23).

So, I encourage you to remember that your parents are not perfect, even if they act like they are!

You cannot judge them or know what they are going through. You know how much you hurt right now, but you will never know how terribly they hurt for themselves and for what they are doing to their children.

Let all bitterness and wrath and anger and clamor and slander be put away from you, along with all malice. Be kind to one another, tenderhearted, forgiving one another, as God in Christ forgave you (Ephesians 4:31–32).

Perhaps once you make it through, you can send me an email and tell me what you did to help cope and make it through.

I know you have the strength to make it through, you just need some pointers and tips.

Believe in your own strength.

Believe in your own resilience.

Children are to parents like seeds planted in the ground. We plant you at birth, water, fertilize and take care of you. And as you grow and blossom, you will bear your own fruit. That fruit will be your children.

CHAPTER 10

SEEING THE LIGHT

Ask God for guidance. When I started my church, I asked God for a name. I vacillated over several names as I tried to name the church. Something catchy. Something memorable. Something personal. Something with my name. Something that would make people want to come. I did not know. Then it simply dropped in my Spirit. God is light. His Son is light. In a world of darkness, it is light that gives people hope. During the winter, people can handle snow, ice, sleet and cold. But what they cannot handle is days upon days with no sun. No light. God said, "House of Light.: Jesus is the light, light of the world. Let your light shine before men. You are a lamp unto my feet and a light unto my path. What was it about light? Light was hope. Light was warmth. Light was a sign of life.

So, even as I started a church named by God as the House of Light, I thought deeply about what light represented in my divorce. I wondered what was my "light" when I was going through my darkest periods of separation, loneliness, anger, confusion, guilt and despair. What gave me hope? What made me want to go on, in spite of the unknown? What made me want to pick myself up and try again? What made me want to be better? What made me want to learn lessons that I would (hopefully) never repeat? What made me want to forgive? What made me want to pay child support on-time? What made me not want to go to war? What, indeed. Or, rather, who?

During the most difficult times of my separation and divorce, I figured it out. It was my children that gave me light. They were my light. Debbie Boone sang a song, a long time ago, called "You Light Up My Life." Google it and read the words of the chorus.

At the end of the day, it was my children that gave me life and hope. It was my children that lit up my days and filled my nights. They were my motivation to be a Dad, even if I was divorced.

When I look back over those times, and ask myself, "What did I need to realize?" The answer was simple: though my happiness is essential, so too is that of my children. It does not work if they are happy and I am miserable. It does not work if I am happy and they are miserable. I needed to find that happy medium. I needed to find that space where I could be a great parent to my children as a result of being whole. I needed to realize that it just doesn't work if I stayed in a marriage and was unhappy, thinking I am doing my children a favor.

Children are smart. They are far more intelligent and intuitive, than we give them credit. If you were in a marriage and were unhappy, I guarantee you your children knew it. They picked up on the vibe. They felt the tension. They may never tell you, but if they ever see you truly happy, they will know it was best for you and their mother to get a divorce.

Part of my motivation for writing this book was the realization that just because you do not live with your children's mother, that does not absolve you from being the best Dad you can be. Too many men divorce their spouse and their children all at once. They think just because the ex is bitter and the children are angry, their best course of action is to walk away and maybe, just maybe, occasionally send some money—or not.

When your children are hurt and angry over the divorce, your Dad cape needs to come out! That is when you need to find your phone booth or bat cave or whatever it is and turn into Super Dad! That is not the time to become the Invisible Man!

Beyond that realization, I also challenged myself to discover what I did not see. What I did not see, during this time was the complete one-sidedness of the way I went about pursuing my own happiness. I did not see the collateral damage of the divorce.

I am embarrassed to say that I was so blind when it came to the impact on my children, I thought to myself, "My children are like me! They are strong. They can get through this. As long as I do not go too far too fast, they will be just fine. They have a lot of me in them, so they are mentally tough!" Ha! The joke was on me.

I did not see the devastating effect this had on my daughter, being that Dads are their daughter's first love. I did not see the devastating effect this had on my son, being that Dads are who their sons want to validate their manhood. But none of that could happen with them being wounded.

Perhaps my children were strong enough to get through it. But at what cost? It was that cost that I did not realize. I just figured they would gut it out. I figured they would be just fine, since so many other children have endured divorce and survived.

What I did not see was the light my children needed in their own lives, as a result of the divorce. What was going to give them hope? What was going to give them warmth and make them want to carry on? I did not see the need to throw my kids a flashlight, or torch or something. I thrust them into darkness and did not think enough of them to give them batteries for their flashlights. Then I had the nerve to be surprised and arrogantly disappointed when they floundered in darkness, with nothing to help move them toward the light or provide any for their steps.

As I sit here writing this, I have tears in my eyes thinking of just how badly I erred in my arrogance and my selfishness. No, if I had it to do all over again, I would not stay married. But, if I had it to do all over again, I would have worked to throw my children a light line. It is so unfair not to do so.

Finally, given all of this, it was my faith that helped me heal and move forward. It was my faith in God and the Word that helped me see the light and understand that I can either regret it therefore allowing it to eat away at me or I could embrace it and pay it forward.

During that time, there were a couple of Scriptures that stuck with me and gave me comfort.

And we know that all that happens to us is working for our good if we love God and are fitting into his plans (Romans 8:28).

I was hurting so badly, but this Scripture helped me understand that somehow, good would come out of this situation. I did not know how. I could not see how. But I knew it had to be the case, because God cannot lie. So, I often meditated on this Scripture and allowed my mind to run wild with all the "good" that was going to one day come my way.

"For I know the plans that I have for you," declares the Lord, "plans for well-being, and not for calamity, in order to give you a future and a hope" (Jeremiah 29:11).

Oh, this Scripture often made me want to curl up and just cry. It spoke directly to me and let me know that God had a plan for my life. All I had to do was make it through this situation. All I had to do was keep him first in my life.

But seek ye first the kingdom of God, and his righteousness; and all these things shall be added unto you (Matthew 6:33).

I knew all I had to do was keep God first and God plan was to prosper me.

....and as long as he sought the Lord, God made him to prosper (2 Chronicles 26:5).

As my journey through divorced progressed from darkness into light, I kept my sight on Hebrews 11:1.

Now faith is the substance of things hoped for, the evidence of things not seen (Hebrews 11:1).

I had hope of a full recovery and the ability to be a great dad to my children. I could not see it. Many days I could not feel it. But I hoped upon hope that it would be the case. I knew good had to come out of this. I knew God had a plan for me that would prosper me. I know I had faith.

As I have progressed in this journey, I never let go of my faith. I never stopped believing that even if I fall down, I can get back up and try again.

> *For a righteous man falls seven times, and rises again. But the wicked stumble in time of calamity* (Proverbs 24:16)

I never stopped believing that the most important thing as a divorced man with children was to be a great dad.

You see, I cannot go back in time and throw my children a light line. I cannot make up for thrusting them into darkness and leaving them groping for an answer. I can ask them to forgive me, I can forgive myself and I can start now doing everything I can to be the Dad they need. But, that is not enough. The Word of God calls us to strengthen others.

> *But I have prayed for thee, that thy faith fail not: and when thou art converted, strengthen thy breth-ren* (Luke 22:32)

This is about strengthening other Dad's so they don't make the same mistakes I made. It is about strengthening other Dad's so they do the right things I did. No, I cannot pay back that stern and unforgiving teacher we call "experience," but I can pay it forward and help other Dads and other children not enter, or remain, in darkness, without the benefit of God's light of revelation and redemption shining on them.

As Dads, we must equip our children for everything they will encounter in life. As we do, we must then fly cover for them as they encounter life's challenges.

Perhaps we will never have to engage. Perhaps we will never need to drop a bomb. Maybe all we need to do is light the way so they can see their targets and their path.

If that is our role, then it is indeed one of honor and one which speaks to us seeing our light and helping them see theirs.

CHAPTER 11

DEAR DADS

By Cidnee J. Gordon

Divorce can be messy. It is the parent's job to make sure it does not hurt the children.

When you become parents, you have the job to keep your children safe. Not just physical safety, but mental safety too. Divorce strains the family so I think that it is the parents that should be responsible for keeping the children mentally safe.

I remember the day, hour, and exactly what I was wearing when my parents sat my brother and me down for the "talk." Instead of hearing about the birds and the bees, as I was expecting, my parents told us they were divorcing.

I was confused because they were together for so long. It was weird because I thought people that got married weren't supposed to get divorced, at least people who were Christians. I wasn't really processing what was going on. I remember the day, but I do not remember how I totally felt. I was numb. I remember everything outside of me, but I cannot remember inside of me other than I was really numb and confused.

I did not get angry at first. But later I got really angry.

I was really angry at both of my parents and God too. At first I was not mad at either of my parents more than the other. It was more of confused anger, like why does it have to happen to me? They should have tried to work it out or something. It was more like a confused anger with my dad more than my mom because I could not figure out how someone could walk away from someone they had been married to for so long. I was trying to figure out what happened and why they got divorced. I started thinking about all the things that had been done and trying to figure out what caused it. Was it another person? Was it me? A part of me really wanted to know why they were getting divorced, but another part of me didn't.

As I look back I realize I could have opened up, talked more about my feelings. More than anything I know what I could have done differently is talk to my dad more instead of mostly talking to my mom.

I was very young. I had just turned twelve years old. Being so young, I really did not understand everything. I was really confused. I had no idea how it would affect my life and I was scared about how it would. This event shook up my entire world. The way my parents told me left me so confused. I really wish they would have agreed to not tell us anything. I really did not want to know. I wanted to know then, but as I look back on it now, I wish they just would have said, "We are splitting up because some people are just not meant for one another and it took us a long time to figure that out." I wish they would have said it together and left it at that. My mother talked about it, while my dad said nothing. I wish they would have just agreed to tell us together, then say nothing more individually. By my father not saying anything, it made me blame him. I faulted him for all the things I felt he did. I didn't understand what was happening. I knew my parents were no longer together, but I didn't understand why.

It was not like they did not argue and like I did not know there were problems. I was not surprised, but I was shocked. The reason is because I just figured they would work things out. That's what adults are supposed to do. They always lecture us on being an adult and on adults making tough decisions and having responsibility and now they were being hypocrites.

So, looking back, I saw all the signs. I heard the arguments and would go to my room and cry when I did. I heard my mother talking to my dad and him just sitting there. I would think, "Why doesn't he say something? Why doesn't he defend himself?" Then I concluded he did not defend himself because he must be guilty of the stuff she was saying. I hated him because he made all this happen to our family. I did not know what this would mean to our family; I just knew I knew other children in my school who said after their parents got divorced things were really different. I started worrying about what would happen after he left. Would we have enough money to live on? Would I have to transfer schools? Would we have to move to a smaller house? Would we have to get a different car? Would I have to have to buy clothes from K-Mart or the Goodwill? I knew a lot of children had to do those things and it is not a bad thing, but I just never thought I would have to do it. I mean my parents owned a Land Rover and a BMW. They built a new house. We vacationed in Aruba. We ate out all the time. My dad would travel and bring me back Coach Purses. But now we were going to be really poor. I kept thinking I was going to have to get free lunch from my school. I hated my dad for making me have to get free lunch.

I wanted answers. Looking back, I wanted answers sort of. I kind of did and I kind of didn't. I was afraid of the answers. How could my dad just walk away? Why wasn't our family enough for him? Why did he have to be so selfish? Why did his marriage vows mean nothing to him? Why didn't my brother I mean more to him? Everything I thought was all about my dad and blaming him. He was my dad, so it had to be his fault. He was silent and never explained or gave us any information. My mom was hurting and crying. My dad was walking around like everything was okay. Why wasn't he crying? Why didn't he act like he was going to miss being a family? Was he a robot? Did he ever really care about us?

Although it can be difficult for your child, here are three steps I think you should take as a father after your divorce:

Step one to being a great dad is to keep your children in a child's place. I would rather have been told the details when I was sixteen or seventeen, instead of when I was twelve. I would have rather had my childhood. I feel like I was forced to grow up. Being a great dad means allowing your children to have their childhood. Do not tell them too much or give them too many details. I am not saying that you have to wait and stay married, but if you are going to break up, then tell your children as little as possible, so they can still be children and stay in a child's place. Being a child, it was not easy to digest. I could not make up my own mind who was telling the truth or who I should believe and trust. I am older now and am just able to better process the divorce. However, when it happened and I was going through it, I was much too young and that made me grow up faster than I wanted.

We grew up listening to older people tell us to 'stay in a child's place,' but not many of us really want to hear that. But now that I have had time to heal after my parent's divorce, I think it is best not to tell your child the reasons why. I strongly feel under absolutely no circumstances should you say anything to your children about their mother or father, why you no longer love them, or how terrible the other person is. Both of you are human and your children love both of you and because of that, any negative comments damage the outlook your child has on the other parent.

The reality for a child who is losing their family is that their parents will lose but the children do not necessarily have to. They should feel like they are still loved and still have parents, their parents are just not living together anymore. That is the best possible reality!

Growing up I was afraid to love anyone and I blamed my hatred for love on the divorce. It was very easy to do. I thought if my parents said they loved each other for seventeen years and broke up, love must not be real. I walked around bitter and sad every day.

Step two to being a great dad is to show them what true respect and love means. No one is perfect and hard times can show just how imperfect we are. It's important that you always respect your spouse in front of your children. Dads, your children look to their mother as one of the most important figures in their life. You cannot tear her down or mistreat her without it scaring your children. Thankfully, my dad always respected my mom.

I noticed this because my dad always talked to my mom nice, did not raise his voice, and did not yell. He never disrespected her. He never called her out of her name. He never did spiteful stuff to her.

I'm sure when he went back to his home he would yell or get angry, but he never let me or my brother see him treating our mom that way. In addition to that, he never talked bad about her to us. Not when she wasn't around. Not when she was. Nothing. He would never retaliate. More than anything, he always would tell her we were the most important things to him and because she was our mother, he would not disrespect her. He told her that. He told her that in front of us. And she never said he was lying or she never said he didn't. Because my mom talked openly and honestly to us, I was sure if he disrespected her when we were not around, she would have said it.

Step three to being a great dad is to spend time with your children after the divorce. It is better if you can spend even more, especially because we are afraid we may never see you again or if we do, it will be for small periods of time. Time, not money, is what is important.

As a child, I enjoyed daddy–daughter dates and watching movies with my father. After the divorce those things stopped. Now my dad was living somewhere else and when I would see him, we did not do any of these things. That hurt me the most because he had no idea how important those things were to me. I guess I should have told him. Yeah, I definitely should have told him. Maybe he did not understand how much they meant to me. As a daughter who idolized her dad and loved spending time with him, these things meant the world to me. And not just these things, but anything that I could do with him mattered and made me feel special. After the divorce, I felt like I stopped feeling special to my dad. Do not try to replace time with money. I mean do not get me wrong, I loved him to give me money or an allowance or to buy me things, but if I had a choice, I would take a Daddy Daughter Dance or a movie night with my dad over anything he could buy me or any money he could give me.

With my Dad, all I wanted to do was sit on the couch, order pizza and watch movies. It was like a joy spending time with my dad because I knew how valuable his time was, how busy he was and how much stuff he had to do. So, when he would spend time with me it made me feel like I was still important to him and I still mattered. I enjoyed the presents, they were special. But over presents I would have just rather gone anywhere with my dad. I remember sometimes he would take me to the mall and just walk around. We would get Cold stone's and sit down and eat it and maybe he would buy me something and maybe he wouldn't. I did not care. Just being there, just walking around with him, just spending time with him made all the difference in the world to me!

My father's effort was everything. He tried and tried and tried to be my father no matter how hurt or in pain I was.

His effort to maintain a strong connection with me eventually made our relationship better. No matter how much I ignored him and how angry I was with him and how much of an attitude I had with him, he kept trying. He did not use my actions against me. He did not use my bad attitudes and anger towards him as an excuse to run away from me. My dad made me feel special by not going away. He could have moved with his job, but instead he chose me.

I remember times when I was at his house and I would shut myself in my room. I was angry at him and told myself I did not want to be there. But my dad would keep smiling and keep trying. He would call me and ask me to come downstairs. He would cook dinner and do things to make me laugh. He would be silly and goofy, and that was really cool. I wanted to hate him, but he refused to let me. I wanted to blame him but he refused to go away like I was so afraid he would. He like really fought for me and my brother, even though we really did not make him think we wanted him to.

Because my dad fought so hard for our relationship, it made me know that is how a guy is supposed to treat you. My dad never laid a hand on me. Even when I deserved a spanking or to be punished he would always say it is not right for a man to put his hands on a woman, whether it is his wife, his daughter or his girlfriend.

I would tell dads to say to their children that no matter what and no matter who comes in or out of my life, no one will ever replace the spot you have in my heart. Just because I am divorcing your mother, I am not divorcing you. You will always be my child, no matter what.

I wish I could quote a Bible Scripture for dads or children, but the truth is at that time, though I considered myself a Christian, I was too young and too immature to understand all of what was going on. I was too young to know that I could pray to God and ask him for strength. I was too young to know God was there with me and that He helped me get through it. I did not know that then, but I know it now. That goes back to my earlier point when I said the parents should wait until the children are older, like sixteen or seventeen. Part of that is because when they are older they understand God can help get them through it.

Back then, I definitely blamed God and gave up on God.

It was like if God was real he would not have let this happen. Around that time, it made it easier to think that way because once my parents separated we stopped going to church. Looking back on it now, I understand that people get divorced every day. I understand I just needed someone to blame and God was a good person because he could not defend himself. The little bit of faith I had from going to church with my dad was shaken and an absence of church helped it to be shaken even more. Even now I am not a great Bible scholar, but there is one Scripture I kept saying to myself and still say to myself when I get down, get into a tough situation or am faced with difficult times. The Scripture is Philippians 4:13, which says, "I can do all this through Him who gives me strength." I repeat that to myself over and over and it gives me hope, makes me strong and makes me know I can get through any tough times. Just like I made it through the divorce of my parents, I can make it through anything.

The last thing I will say to fathers is I hope you are as persistent as my dad and it is as important to have a relationship with your children as it was for my dad to have one with us. I hope you are willing to go through the anger, blame, bad treatment, petty treatment and whatever it takes to be a great dad. Your children are angry and confused. Do not take it personal. Your children really love you and want a relationship with you, they just need to know you still love them, will love them and will be around to love them. Convince them of that and you will have children that adore you like I adore my Knight-in-Shining Armor dad.

EPILOGUE

I learned many lessons from my mistakes. I can honestly say I am still learning and still making mistakes. Raising children is not easy, but it is definitely worth it.

As I look at my children, I struggle with what I should say and what I should do. The one thing for sure is that there is no manual.

> *Train up a child in the way he should go: and when he is old, he will not depart from it* (Proverbs 22:6).

But, who determines the way a child should go? Where is that written?

Based on my experience raising children, the insight I have gleaned from others, my general acumen and expertise on the subject as a pastor and counselor, the way a child should go is parallel with the way we should go. A child should be raised to love the Lord and love others.

> *Jesus said unto him, Thou shalt love the Lord thy God with all thy hearty and with all thy soul, and with all thy mind. This is the first and great commandment. And the second is like unto it, Thou shalt love thy neighbor as thyself* (Matthew 22:37–39).

If you can raise your child to do those two things, they will be okay, as this is the essence of what is asked of us by God.

As I think along the lines of the way things "should go," I would like to end this book with a few words of encouragement:

To the Men

As you travel the road of divorce, whether you initiated the paperwork or it was presented to you, you still have a responsibility to your children. You must still be a man and you must still be provider, protector and priest. As you look forward, you must use your 20/20 Character Vision and stay away from using your "I-sight."

Yes, it will be hard some days. Your emotions will feel raw and you are going to be tempted to go to war. But, when those thoughts cross your mind, picture a battle torn landscape: black, barren, smoking, void of vegetation or life. That will be your children on the inside, if you fight unnecessary wars and attack the other half of what makes them who they are.

In all you do, keep God first and keep your children lifted up in prayer. Seek therapy and allow the grieving process to take its full term. Remember your children need a healthy man to lead them and provide for them. Anger is acceptable and even expected, but don't use it to sin.

In your anger do not sin (Ephesians 4:26).

Do not sin by murdering your children's mother's influence or reputation. Do not steal your children-mother's relationships.

The bottom line is no matter what, do not allow your children to become a casualty of the divorce. Divorce your ex, if you must, but never divorce your children and your responsibility to them.

To the Women

Recently I counseled a man who is divorced. He was broken. He was devastated. He had been reduced to a shell of a man. What happened to him? Why was he this way?

It was because he believed his ex-wife used their children as a weapon. She poisoned their children and told them sordid stories of this man's past. She showed them text messages he sent her in anger.

She did all she could to ensure there was not, and would never be, a relationship between this man and his daughters.

I have not counseled her and do not know her story. But here is what I know:

> *Be not deceived: evil communications corrupt good manners* (1 Corinthians 15:33).

No woman or man has the right to poison children against a parent. No woman has the right to keep her children from their father. No woman has the right to use children as a point of leverage to make a man do what she wants. No woman has a right to refuse a man's access to his children, save for physical safety concerns. While the majority of women are the custodial parent, this premise still holds true for men and how they interact with their children regarding their mothers. I have seen men try to poison their children against the mother. I have seen men attempt to turn their children against their own mother—the woman that carried them for nine months, nurtured them, and in many cases was there for them constantly, both physically and mentally. So, there is certainly no monopoly on trying to turn children against the other parent. But no matter how you slice it and no matter who does it, it is absolutely not acceptable. It is not Godly. And, it is deleterious to the children. This is equally true for men and how they interact with their children regarding their mothers. No matter how you slice it, it's just not acceptable or Godly.

This man I counseled said he never abused his daughters. He said he was never inappropriate or immoral with them. He acknowledged he sent text messages to their mother, intended for her and done at a time when he was very emotional (…remember the chapter on emotions?).

In other words, the man did not fancy himself as blameless. But he did fancy himself as a father who desperately missed his daughters. He now struggles with depression and guilt. He is fighting to maintain his self-esteem and dignity.

I shared that story as a reminder to the women who read this book. Do not use your children as weapons of mass destruction (WMDs) against your ex. No matter how badly he hurt you. No matter how much he lied. No matter how much you now hate him. No matter what he did that suggests he does not care about his children or his family.

Do not bring your children into the fight. Do not use your children as WMDs.

I try very hard when I counsel not to insert myself, my experiences or my personal reflections. I try to always remember that each person is different, each person processes differently and each person responds differently. Therefore, I am careful not to view their circumstances through my own lens. However, in this case, I feel compelled to wade into the forbidden waters, I typically avoid.

[Putting on my lenses]

As a man with children, it would devastate me if my children were used as WMDs. There is no greater weapon against a man than to turn his children against him. It is akin to refusing sex to a married man. It is the ultimate weapon and hits far below the belt. Men, like women, look for love— acceptance, approval, and validation from their children—no different than the children look receive the same from their fathers. Hence, when it is withheld or even worse, turned to outright disapproval, disownment, or disdain, then its effects are crippling. I am sure this is why it is used by men and women alike. You can make more money. You can buy more stuff. You can get another house. But, you cannot make another child like the one you have. Yes, you can have more children, but each child is unique and a father knows and understands their uniqueness, like no one else, save their own mother.

As I reflect on the gentleman's situation, I can state without qualification, it would tear me apart to be refused access to my children or to have my children purposely and / or provocatively turned against me.

The primary reason for this is that beyond contestation, the love I have for my children is not limited by the circumstances of my divorce. I do not believe I am alone in this feeling. In spite of outward appearances, ill-advised behavior, or unfortunate actions, men love their children deeply and supremely.

While their love may not look, smell or taste like a mother's love, a man is not ordered by God to be like the woman in PROVERBS 31, rather is ordered to be like David towards his son Absalom in 2 Samuel 18:33.

> *The tongue can bring death or life; those who love to talk will reap the consequences* (Proverbs 18:21).

Do not kill your ex in the eyes of his children. In your opinion, he may not be a "real man." He may not be provider, protector or priest. He may be wrong and terrible. However, as God extends grace to us, I ask you to extend grace to him, understanding that anyone can be redeemed.

> *Forgive us our debts, as we forgive our debtors* (Matthew 6:12).

> *For judgment is without mercy to one who has shown no mercy. Mercy triumphs over judgment* (James 2:13).

Please read the story of the debtor, who owed to a king in Matthew 18:21–35. While I do not wish to intimate whose sins are greater, God calls upon us to forgive and to show mercy, even as he forgives us and has shown us mercy.

Sometimes it takes drastic events to wake a person up. Those events are not yours to impart. You are not the one to judge. Only God can judge.

As I have admonished, encouraged and informed men throughout this book, I would ask you to work with me and my counsel and pray for your children's father. Be vigilant, wise and full of grace. If your children's father wants to be part of their lives, thank God he does and find another way to convince him to do the things you feel are necessary to address his responsibility.

Again, I am not suggesting you subject yourself or your children to someone who is abusive or dangerous. However, if the issue is not concerning physical safety, then I ask you not to use your children as WMDs. There are many men who want their children in their lives, but do not want you.

While this may be distasteful and painful, for the sake of the children, figure out a way to make it about the children and not about what hurts your feelings or upsets you. As I stated to the men repeatedly, it is not about the two of you, it is about your children. They deserve a chance to find happiness, despite the divorce of their parents and this can never happen if you use them as pawns.

Let me pause for a moment and remind men that despite whatever obstacle you may face, as it relates to being a dad to your children, you are called to endure hardship like a good soldier. You are called to figure it out. You are called to adapt and adjust. You are called to overcome. If it was easy, then boys could do it. But it is not easy and it takes a man. Be that man. Do not hide in excuses. Do not be easily defeated by someone who is hurting and primarily lashing out in response to your actions. Do not yield to defeat. Your relationship with your children is the prize and they are counting on you to be the victor.

Yes, it is hard, tough, demanding and exhausting. But you are their Dad. You are not merely a man. Rip off those clothes and reveal the D on your chest! Go into your phone booth or your bat cave and morph into the cape-wearing, muscle-bound, tights-sporting super hero that can leap tall objections in a single bound—that can catch fiery darts in his teeth; that can stop a speeding lie in its tracks. Be that superhero your children need. It is easy to make excuses and buckle under the weight of a difficult task, but God is calling you to be provider, protector and priest.

God is calling you to remember that,

> *The race is not to the swift or the battle to the strong*
> (Ecclesiastes 9:11).

And,

but the one who endures to the end will be saved
(Matthew 24:13).

Endure. Your children are worth it.

At the end of the day, your children deserve a father who is Divorced, But Still Dad.

ACKNOWLEDGEMENTS

First and foremost, I want to thank God, who is full of grace and mercy. He is my savior, my redeemer and my provider. If it were not for Him, I would not have been inspired to write this book and would not have had the ability to address a subject that so clearly pointed out my failures, yet gives hope to others. If it were not for Him I would not have been given the chance, through grace, to fail forward.

Thank you to my beautiful angel, my lover, my friend, and my wife. Leslie, you give me courage, inspire me to be a better person and make me happier than I have ever been.

Thank you to my Mom and Dad, who have been married over fifty years and have modeled how a wonderful marriage is supposed to look. Thank you to my Dad, who is the greatest example of a man a boy, could ever have and the greatest example of a Dad a father could ever have.

Thank you to my children, KT and Cidnee, for showing me what it means to love and be loved unconditionally. Thank both of you for teaching me what it means to be a Dad and for having patience with me as I work to be the Dad you deserve.

Thank you to my family for all your support and assistance with my children as you stood in the gap for me countless times.

Thank you Aunt Von and Auntie for all you did for the Appaloosas! Thank both of you for being taxis, therapists, ATMs, Homeschoolers, and confidantes. Thank you for babysitting, teen sitting and house sitting.

Thank you Val and Neisy for treating my children like your brother and sister and not your cousins. Thank you for all you did for and with them, from the homework tutoring to the encouraging guidance.

Thank you Mom and Dad for being awesome Grandparents. You gave my children more than money could ever purchase. While you gave them amazing gifts at Christmas, for their birthdays and "just because" you also poured into them things money cannot buy, such as character, identity, pride and knowledge of God. Your contributions to my children will never be forgotten!

Thank you to my children's mother for giving me two wonderful children. Thank you for allowing our focus to always stay on what is best for our children.

Thank you to my friend, Hezekiah Griggs III for inspiring me and enabling me as I shared the vision and dream of this book. Thank you for your wisdom, guidance and perspective. You were living proof that young people can have old Spirits and lots of wisdom.

APPENDIX

Abbrev.

Forward
Proverbs 13:22 KJV
2 Corinthians 6:14 KJV
Ephesians 4:32 ESV
Deuteronomy 6:7 KJV
Proverbs 22:6 KJV
Deuteronomy 23:14 NIV
Introduction
2 Peter 3:18 NIV
2 Timothy 3:16 KJV
Joshua 24:15 KJV

Chapter 1
Proverbs 18:22 AKJV
Proverbs 31:10–13 NIV
Hebrews 13:4 KJV
Flint Water Crisis [source: Wikipedia]
Ephesians 4:26 ISV

Chapter 2
Romans 8:28 KJV
Philippians 4:13 NIV
I Samuel 30:6 KJV
David and Goliath, I Samuel 17 KJV
Jeremiah 29:11 NIV

Matthew 6:33 KJV

Appointment with Love by S.I. Kishor, adapted and updated by Ken Gordon

Tell me whom you love, Arsene Houssaye

Chapter 3

"Those who cannot remember the past are condemned to repeat it" George Santayana (1905)

Reason in Common Sense, Vol. 1 of The Life of Reason.

Luke 9:26 NIV

"Brick House" by The Commodores [source: Wikipedia]

I Samuel 16:7 NASB

Proverbs 4:23 NIV

"To understand the heart and mind of a person, look not at what he has already achieved, but what he aspires to."

Become a Conscious Creator: A Return to Self-Empowerment (2007)

6th sense simple definition [source: Merriam-Webster's L.D.]

Mark 8:25 Berean Study Bible

Chapter 4

The 5 Stages of Grief: On Death and Dying, [source: Wikipedia]

Mark 10:11–12 NIV

Malachi 2:16 NIV

Deuteronomy 24:1 NIV

John 4:3-NIV Mark 1:14 NIV

Matthew 4:12 NIV

John 18 NIV Luke 23 NIV

Genesis 3:16 KJ2000 Bible

Ephesians 6:4 NASB

1 Corinthians 11:3 NASB

Ephesians 5:22–23 ESV

Albert (known as Mr.) – Mr. is the man to whom Celie is married in the movie adaption of The Color Purple. Originally, he seeks a relationship with Celie's sister, Nettie but eventually settles for Celie. Mr. mistreats Celie just as her stepfather had, although Celie does not understand that she doesn't have to tolerate the

DIVORCED, BUT STILL DAD

abuse. Mr. uses Celie to help raise his children, who give her a hard time because she is not their biological mother. When Shug Avery, a blues singer, comes to town, Mr. falls for her and makes her his mistress. Through Shug's seductive and manipulative influence, Mr. begins to treat Celie better. In the end, Mr. realizes he has mistreated Celie and seeks a friendship with her.

The Color Purple – a 1982 epistolary novel by American author Alice Walker that won the 1983 Pulitzer Prize for Fiction and the National Book Award for Fiction. It was later adapted into a film and musical of the same name. Taking place mostly in rural Georgia, the story focuses on the life of African-American women in the southern United States in the 1930s, addressing numerous issues including their exceedingly low position in American social culture. The novel has been the frequent target of censors and appears on the American Library Association list of the 100 Most Frequently Challenged Books of 2000–2009 at number seventeen because of the sometimes-explicit content, particularly in terms of violence.

Hebrews 6:10 KJV

Chapter 5

Man—one possessing in high degree the qualities considered distinctive of manhood—the quality or state of being manly an adult male human being; a man or boy who shows the qualities (such as strength and courage) that men are traditionally supposed to have; a woman's husband or boyfriend, [source: Merriam—Webster's L.D.]

Psychology of Men http://www.psychologyofmen.org/

Genesis 3:19 NIY

Genesis 3:19 Matthew Henry's Commentary

1 Peter 3:7 KJV

Dr. Eddie I. Hyatt - "Why the Woman as the Weaker Vessel Teaching is Wrong" - Charisma Magazine - April 15, 2015

Letter from Birmingham Jail - The Letter from Birmingham Jail, also known as the Letter from Birmingham City Jail and The Negro Is Your Brother, is an open letter written on April 16,

1963, by Martin Luther King, Jr. The letter defends the strategy of nonviolent resistance to racism. It says that people have
a moral responsibility to break unjust laws and to take direct
action rather than waiting potentially forever for justice to
come through the courts. Responding to being referred to as an
"outsider," King writes, "Injustice anywhere is a threat to justice
everywhere." The letter was widely published and became an
important text for the American Civil Rights Movement during
the early 1960s.

Genesis 1:27–28 KJV

Genesis 3:12 KJV

Genesis 3:6 KJV

Jimmy Choos – Datuk Jimmy Choo, OBE Jimmy Choo Yeang
Keat (Chinese: JpHiP?fc; pinyin: Zhou Yangjie), (born 15
November) is a Malaysian fashion designer based in the United
Kingdom. He is best known for co-founding Jimmy Choo Ltd
that became known for its handmade women's shoes [source:
http://us.jimmychoo.com]

Manolo Blahniks – Manuel "Manolo" Blahnik Rodriguez CBE
(born 27 November 1942, Santa Cruz de La Palma, Spain), is a
Spanish fashion designer and founder of the self-named, high-
end shoe brand [source: https://www.manoloblahnik.com]

Christian Louboutins – French: [kKis.tja lu.bu.te]; born 7 January
1963, is a French luxury footwear and fashion designer whose
footwear has incorporated shiny, red-lacquered soles that have
become his signature [source: http://us.christianlouboutin.
com]

Miu Mius – an Italian high fashion women's clothing and acces-
sory brand and a fully owned subsidiary of Prada. It is headed
by Miuccia Prada and headquartered in Milan, Italy [source:
http://www.miumiu.com]

Walter Steigers a French shoe company, founded in Geneva in 1932
by Walter Steiger senior, making made-to-measure shoes for
men and women [source: http://us.waitersteiger.corm]

1 Corinthians 11:3 NIV

Chapter 6
"Why Divorce Hurts" by Dr. Andra Brosh,
September 14, 2012 [source: Goodreads]
Helen Fischer "Why We Love" [source: Goodreads]
Oklahoma Sooners [source: Wikipedia]

Chapter 7
Deuteronomy 6:6–7 NASB
Joel 1:3-NASB Psalms 78:4 NASB
Proverbs 22:6 NASB
1 Timothy 5:8 NASB
"The Role of Parents in Children's Psychological
Development" by Jerome Kagan, PhD, PEDIATRICS Vol. 104
No. 1 July 1999
Proverbs 22:6 NASB
Romans 14:19 NASB
Van Schaick & Stolberg, 2001 "The Impact of Paternal Involvement
    and Parental Divorce on Young Adults' Intimate Relationships",
    Journal of Divorce & Remarriage 36(1–2):99-121 November
    2001 [source: ResearchGate.net]
Tayler, Parker & Roy, 1995 - "Long-Term Effects of Parental Divorce
    on Love Relationships: Divorce as Attachment Disruption",
    Journal of Social and Personal Relationships 15(1):23–38
    January 1998 [source: ResearchGate.net]
Maccoby & Mnookin, 1992 – America's Fathers and Public Policy:
    Report of a Workshop - National Research Council (US) and
    Institute of Medicine (US) Board on Children and Families;
    Crowell NA, Leeper EM, editors. Washington (DC): National
    Academies Press (US); 1994
[source: http://www.ncbi.nlm.nih.gov/books/NBK231400]
Romans 2:6 - Berean Study Bible
Psalms 127:3–5 ESV
2 Samuel 13:39 KJV
2 Samuel 16:22 ISV
2 Samuel 18:5 KJV
Exodus 20:12 KJV

2 Samuel 18:33 NIV

"How Dads Affect Their Daughters into Adulthood" by Linda Nielsen [source: Family-studies.org]

"The importance of the father-daughter relationship" by Elizabeth Weiss McGolerick - October 11, 2012

"Divorce - What Girls Miss When Dad Leaves The Home", by Erika Krull, MS, LMHP - 7 Feb 2013

"Cat's in the Cradle" – a 1974 folk rock song by Harry Chapin from the album Verities & Balderdash. The song is told in the first-person by a father who is too busy with work to spend time with his son. Each time the son asks him to join in childhood activities, the father issues vague promises of spending time together in the future. While disappointed, the son accepts his excuses and yearns to "be like you, Dad." The first verse tells of his absence at his son's birth and walking, as "there were planes to catch and bills to pay;" the second verse relates the father buying the son a baseball as a birthday present but likewise declining to play catch. The final two verses reverse the roles. In the third verse, the son returns home from college and his father finally has some time to spend with him. Instead, the son just wants to go out and asks the father for the car keys. The fourth verse advances the story quite some time, when the father is long retired and his son has started his own family some distance away. The father makes a phone call to his son and invites him for a visit, but the son has his own issues with his job and his children are sick with "the flu." He tells his father he will visit him if he "can find the time" and says "it's been sure nice talking to you" before he says goodbye. The final two lines of the song reflect the father's observation of what has happened: his son had turned out just like him. The song's chorus references several childhood things: The Cat's in the Cradle string game, silver spoons that are given to babies as christening gifts, and the nursery rhymes Little Boy Blue and Man in the Moon.

Ephesians 6:1–3 NASB

Deuteronomy 6:6–7 NASB

Chapter 8
1 Corinthians 7:9 ESV
Proverbs 18:22 ESV
2 Corinthians 6:14–15 ESV
Matthew 22:37 Berean Study Bible
Matthew 6:33 ESV
Proverbs 3:5–6 ESV
1 Corinthians 10:23 NIV
Ecclesiastes 3:1–8 NIV
Romans 14:19 ESV
"Dating After Divorce" [source: DivorceHelpforparents.org]
"Dating, Divorce & Your Kids" by Helen Setrakian, M.A. [source:
    eHarmony.com] 4 Kinds of Greek Love [source: Wikipedia]
"When Should Divorced Dads Introduce The New Girlfriend?" by
    By Tara Lynne Groth, DadsDivorce™ A service of Cordell &
    Cordell, P.C.
Proverbs 3:6 KJV

Chapter 9
Matthew 5:7 ESV
Luke 6:31 NIV
Galatians 6:7 NIV
Acts 20:24 NIV
Ephesians 2:8–9 NIV
Romans 3:23 NIV
1 Peter 5:5 NIV
Ephesians 1:5–6 NIV
Matthew 6:12 NIV
Proverbs 4:7 KJV
Proverbs 15:1 NIV
John 8:32 ESV
127 Hours – a 2010 British–American biographical survival drama
    film directed, cowritten, and produced by Danny Boyle.
James 3:2 - ISV
Romans 3:23 - NIV
Ephesians 4:31–32 ESV

Chapter 10

"You Light Up My Life" - (1977) was the first solo album from singer
    Debby Boone. It was written by Joseph "Joe" Brooks.

Romans 8:28 TLB

Jeremiah 29:11 ISV

Matthew 6:33 ESV

2 Chronicles 26:5 ESV

Hebrews 11:1 KJV

Proverbs 24:16 NASB

Luke 22:32 KJV

Chapter 11

Philippians 4:13 NIV

Epilogue

Proverbs 22:6 KJV

Matthew 22:37–39 KJV

Ephesians 4:26 NIV

1 Corinthians 15:33 KJV

Proverbs 31 NIV

2 Samuel 18:33 ISV

Proverbs 18:21 NLT

Matthew 6:12 KJV

James 2:13 ESV

Matthew 18:21–3 5 NIV

Ecclesiastes 9:11 NIV

Matthew 24:13 NLT

POSTSCRIPT

One last thing. I need to recommend to all dads, especially those who are divorced:

Hugs, kisses and "I love yous." Okay, that's it.

Please provide each of those three in generous portions to all your children, female and male (Yes, Dads, equally to your male children as well!). You cannot hug, kiss or say I love you enough to your children.

You would be surprised, sadly so, how many children have never heard their father tell them they love them or if they have, only on limited or "special" occasions. Too many children have never had their father hug or kiss them.

Hug your children regardless of your marital status. Kiss your children. Tell your children you love them. Do so every day! Children can never get too much of that.

DADS OF FAITH

Dads of Faith is the online home of Rev. Dr. Ken Gordon Jr.'s initiative to connect fathers with their children utilizing faith-based principles. His latest book, *Divorced, But Still Dad* is the first step in Dr. Gordon's outreach.

Learn more online: www.DadsOfFaith.com

ABOUT THE AUTHOR

REV. DR. KEN GORDON JR. is an accomplished pastor, business executive, and community leader. His entire life has been dedicated to the service of others. A graduate of the prestigious Citadel, he is a highly sought-after speaker on leadership, public service and civil rights, youth mentoring, and community engagement.

In 2016, Dr. Gordon and his wife, Leslie, founded the House of Light Church in Burlington, NJ where they established their Divorce Ministry. The couple, now living in Birmingham, AL, seeks to continue God's work for Divorced and Separated men and women. Learn more about their Divorce Ministry and their church, The House of Light, at www.hoflchurch.org.

Dr. Gordon has two children Ken III and Cidnee from a previous marriage, and is married to Leslie Gordon who also has two children Craig & Christopher from a previous marriage.